Real Estate Exam Prep

Texas

Sherry Steele and John Mathis,
Contributing Editors

This publication is designed to provide accurate and authoritative information in regard to the subject matter covered. It is sold with the understanding that the publisher is not engaged in rendering legal, accounting, or other professional advice. If legal advice or other expert assistance is required, the services of a competent professional should be sought.

President: Dr. Andrew Temte
Chief Learning Officer: Dr. Tim Smaby
Executive Director, Real Estate Education: Melissa Kleeman-Moy
Development Editor: Evonna Burr

TEXAS REAL ESTATE EXAM PREP
©2014 Kaplan, Inc.
Published by DF Institute, Inc., d/b/a Kaplan Real Estate Education
332 Front St. S., Suite 501
La Crosse, WI 54601

Printed in the United States of America

ISBN: 978-1-4754-2565-9 / 1-4754-2565-1
PPN: 2135-9604

Contents

Introduction

When you bought this book, you showed that you were serious about passing the exam and getting your real estate license. This book will help prospective licensees be "scrupulous and meticulous in performing the agent's functions" (Rules Section 531.1(3)) and able to "exercise judgment and skill in the performance of the work" (Rules Section 531.3(3)).

If you practice and review key material, your test score will improve. This book is your key to exam success. The process is simple: Work your way through the true/false questions (see how to complete below).

The content outline features references to specific sections of Texas state law, including the following:

- Texas Occupations Code TRELA Section 1101: Real Estate Brokers and Salespersons (the Real Estate License Act, or TRELA)
- Texas Occupations Code Section 1102: Real Estate Inspectors
- Texas Occupations Code Section 1103: Real Estate Appraisers
- Texas Administrative Code Title 22, Part 23, Sections 531–537: Rules of the Texas Real Estate Commission (or "Rules")

Also featured are a few references to the Deceptive Trade Practices Act (DTPA) and various other state and federal laws. Use these references as an additional resource in your studies.

Getting ready for exam prep—completing true/false questions

Once you have completed the national portion of the course (*Modern Real Estate Practice/Texas Real Estate Principles*), you should start working on the true/false questions in the back of your *National Exam Prep* book. You should be doing these in conjunction with completing the Texas-specific course work.

The exam prep books are divided into two sections. The front is the outline we will be covering in the actual exam prep course, once you have completed all the course work. The back (second) section includes true/false questions on each section of the license exam. These should be completed **before you start exam prep using the method below.** The purpose of starting and completing these questions now is to allow you time to find the areas you may be weak in and give you time to restudy them before exam prep.

How to complete the true/false questions:

1. Use the table of contents to find the back section with the true/false questions in both of your books.
2. Start the section by covering the answers on the right side with a piece of paper and trying to determine whether the statement is true or false.

3. If the statement is false, see if you can change the information to make it a true statement.

For example:

1. Texas is a country in South America.	**F** Texas is a state in the United States in North America.

Your answer should have been false, and you should have been able to change it to the correct answer. If you knew the statement was false but could not come up with the correct answer, this question should be marked as missed.

4. Complete all questions in a section, marking those you do not know. Use the books from the courses to review any areas where you missed a number of questions in (e.g., if you missed all the freehold estate questions, you would go back and study that area).

5. Once you have completed all the true/false questions, retake **only** those you got wrong. If you miss them again, mark them a second, third, or fourth time. Continue doing **only** the questions you miss each time until you completely understand all the concepts and test points and don't miss any questions in the book.

6. The key is to always study what you do **NOT** know until you learn it.

Once you have completed half of your state courses, you should have finished the national true/false questions and be ready to start on the *Texas Exam Prep* book.

Note: We have found that our students who complete all true/false questions using this method get 80 to 90% of their answers correct on the pre-test and post-test exam prep tests. They are also ready to take and pass the state license exam the first time.

Texas Real Estate Licensing Examination

Since 1996, the Texas Real Estate Commission (TREC) has routinely contracted with a national company to provide examination services. Currently, the contract is with Pearson VUE. Regardless of the contractor, the exams for broker and salesperson licensing in Texas consist of both a national and a state portion. Both portions are multiple choice in format, yet objective in nature, and therefore call for a particular method for exam preparation strategy. Ultimately, the salesperson applicant must pass both national and state portions of the exam with a score of at least 70%. A broker applicant must pass with 75%. Although the content outline is the same for both broker and salesperson, the salesperson exam is less exacting and stringent than the broker exam.

Examination Summary Table

Examination	Portion	# of Items	# Correct to Pass	Time Allowed
Salesperson	National	80	56	150 minutes
	State	30	21	90 minutes
	Both	110	77	240 minutes
Broker	National	80	60	150 minutes
	State	40	30	90 minutes
	Both	120	90	240 minutes

The topics on the state portion of the exam are listed in the following paragraphs, along with the number of questions covered by the topic on the salesperson exam and the broker exam.

Commission Duties and Powers (Salesperson, Two Items; Broker, Three Items)

1. General powers: composition, duties, and powers; real estate advisory committees
2. Handling of complaints: investigations, hearings, and appeals
3. Penalties for violation: unlicensed activity; authority for disciplinary actions; recovery trust account

Licensing (Salesperson, Two Items; Broker, Four Items)

1. Activities requiring license: scope of practice; exemptions; business entities; nonresident broker; inspectors and appraisers
2. Licensing process: general requirements (moral character, residency, sponsor, etc.); education; examination; grounds to reject application; appeals of denial, criminal background check (broker only)
3. License maintenance and renewal: continuing education; place of business; change of salesperson sponsorship; inactive status, assumed names

Standards of Conduct (Salesperson, Seven Items; Broker, Nine Items)

1. Professional ethics and conduct
2. Grounds for suspension and revocation
3. Unauthorized practice of law
4. Trust accounts
5. Splitting fees (versus permissible rebates)
6. Advertising rules

Agency/Brokerage (Salesperson, Eight Items; Broker, Ten Items)

1. Disclosure
2. Intermediary practice
3. Duties to client (including minimum services)
4. Enforcing compensation agreements (broker only)
5. Broker-salesperson relationships; broker's responsibility for acts of salesperson
6. Appropriate use of unlicensed assistants

Contracts (Salesperson, Seven Items; Broker, Eight Items)

1. Use and understanding of standard contract forms
2. Statute of frauds
3. Seller disclosure requirements

Special Topics (Salesperson, Four Items; Broker, Six Items)

1. Community property
2. Homestead
3. Deceptive Trade Practices Act
4. Wills and estates
5. Landlord-tenant issues
6. Foreclosure and short sales
7. Recording statutes
8. Mechanics' and materialmen's liens
9. Veterans Land Board
10. Homeowners associations

Score Reports

Candidates receive their scores at the test center immediately after they complete the examination, as well as a diagnostic report indicating strengths and weaknesses. An official paper score report is printed at the examination site.

In order to receive a passing score, candidates must correctly answer a certain minimum number of questions. Note that the minimum passing scores are different for salesperson and broker candidates.

If a candidate passes one portion of the test and not the other, the candidate retakes only the portion of the exam that was not passed. The cost is the same for one or both parts. Exam scores are only valid for three years.

Examination Format

The questions are in the form of four-answer multiple-choice items.

Example: The purpose of requiring a prospective licensee to take an examination is to

1. keep people out of the business.
2. determine the competency of an individual to practice real estate.
3. see if the licensee is good at taking a test.
4. generate revenue from test fees.

The salesperson's exam is less difficult than the broker's exam. The broker's exam is designed to test the applicant in greater detail and application of concepts and includes information indicative of that licensee's practice.

Preparing for the Exam

Courses required for licensure are not designed to *teach the test*. The purpose of courses required by TREC is to develop a fundamental knowledge of real estate. However, the information presented to the reader, enhanced by that presented by the instructor, is the basis of the material that should be studied to pass the license exam. The best way to prepare for the exam is to become thoroughly familiar with the material, particularly what the information means, rather than to memorize. Combining facts and principles and applying that knowledge to real-life situations is needed to pass the exam. Download the *Texas Real Estate Candidate Handbook* at www.pearsonvue.com/tx/realestate/.

Taking the Exam

For best results, first go through the entire examination and answer only those questions about which you are certain, leaving the others for later. After all the questions you know are answered, return to the remaining questions. There is no penalty for guessing; guess if you are unable to arrive at an answer. Remain relaxed. If you are prepared and have an adequate knowledge of the subject, you should be able to complete the exam successfully.

■ EXAM PREP STRENGTH AND WEAKNESS INDICATOR CHART

To use this chart, enter the number you answered correctly in each topic area. For the topics you need to work on, use the page references to go back and review the content in the book.

SP = Salesperson; BK = Broker

Questions Answered Correctly	Topic Area	Exam Prep T/F Items	Exam Prep Outline	Location in Texas Courses
Pre-Test _____ Post-Test _____	Commission Duties and Powers (SP 2 questions; BK 3 questions)	pp. 41–42	pp. 1–6	Texas Real Estate Principles
Pre-Test _____ Post-Test _____	Licensing (SP 2 questions; BK 4 questions)	pp. 43–46	pp. 7–13	Texas Real Estate Principles
Pre-Test _____ Post-Test _____	Standards of Conduct (SP 7 questions; BK 9 questions)	pp. 47–53	pp. 14–18	Texas Real Estate Principles
Pre-Test _____ Post-Test _____	Agency/Brokerage (SP 8 questions; BK 10 questions)	pp. 54–59	pp. 19–24	Texas Law of Agency
Pre-Test _____ Post-Test _____	Contracts (SP 7 questions; BK 8 questions)	pp. 60–65	pp. 25–32	Texas Law of Contracts and Texas Promulgated Forms
Pre-Test _____ Post-Test _____	Special Topics (SP 4 questions; BK 6 questions)	p. 66–72	pp. 33–39	Texas Real Estate Principles

Total Pre-Test

_____

Total Post-Test

_____

*If you answered at least 24 questions (out of 30) correct, you achieved a score of at least 80%.

■ WHAT SHOULD YOU DO IF YOU SCORE 80% OR HIGHER ON THE PRE-TEST?

If You Score 80% or Higher on the Pre-Test. You're doing well, but you may still need to focus on a few areas that you haven't quite mastered. You should do the following:

■ Use the Exam Prep Strength and Weakness Indicator Chart to identify the areas you still need to review.
■ Attend the Exam Prep lectures or view them online, paying special attention to your weak areas.
■ Take the Exam Prep Post-Test at the end of the course.

■ WHAT SHOULD YOU DO IF YOU SCORE LESS THAN 80% ON THE PRE-TEST?

If You Score 75 to 79% on the Pre-Test. You're doing well, but you may need to focus on a few areas that you haven't quite mastered. You should do the following:

■ Use the Exam Prep Strength and Weakness Indicator Chart to identify the areas you most need to review.
■ Attend the Exam Prep lectures or view them online, paying special attention to your weak areas.
■ Take the Exam Prep Post-Test at the end of the course if you are ready; if not, wait and take it when you feel prepared.

If you have already scheduled your exam, evaluate whether you will have enough time to study after the Exam Prep course or if you should reschedule the exam.

If You Score Less Than 75% on the Pre-Test. Students who score below 75% on the Pre-Test generally struggle to pass the actual licensing exam. But don't panic; you can pass it with more study.

- Consider waiting to complete Exam Prep. Often, spending additional time studying and completing or reviewing all the true/false questions will allow you to pass the Post-Test. If you decide that you want to wait, give yourself enough time to study and prepare (typically no more than 3 to 4 weeks). If you have already set a test date, remember you might need to cancel or reschedule it.
- Consult your Exam Prep Strength and Weakness Indicator Chart. This chart will help you identify the content areas in which you need to improve. Start your review with your weakest area first.
- Review real estate terms. Familiarity with real estate terms is crucial. If you're taking Kaplan's complete licensing program, review the key terms in your study materials. If you do not know a term, make a flashcard for yourself. Once you have completed the process, you will have a stack of flashcards to review. If you are not enrolled in Kaplan's entire licensing program, consider purchasing a good real estate dictionary. We have the best books in the industry available for sale on our website and at some of our school locations.
- Study the true/false questions in your Exam Prep book. You've probably reviewed these before, but try answering them again. If you've followed the preceding steps, the concepts tested in the true/false questions will be more familiar. Be sure to conceal the answers as you study the questions. For every false statement, try to change the information to make it a true statement. This will further ensure that you understand the concept being tested.

■ WHAT SHOULD YOU DO IF YOU SCORE LESS THAN 80% ON THE POST-TEST?

If You Score Less Than 80% on Either Portion of the Post-Test. The Post-Test is an accurate predictor of whether you're prepared to pass the actual licensing exam. Scores lower than 80% generally indicate you are not yet ready for the actual exam.

- You need to review the material. If you're enrolled in Kaplan's complete licensing program, reread the relevant units in your materials, attend (or view online) selected class sessions, and work through the review exams until you're ready to try the Post-Test again. Review all the sections and areas you missed using the Exam Prep Strength and Weakness Indicator Chart. Review the true/false questions for those areas.
- When you feel ready, retake the exam.

■ WE ARE HERE TO HELP

The faculty and staff at Kaplan Professional Schools are committed to your success on the licensing exam. Please contact us at any time throughout your studies to let us know how you are doing or how we may be of service.

Commission Duties and Powers

(Test questions: Salesperson, 2; Broker, 3)

I.   THE TEXAS REAL ESTATE COMMISSION (TREC)

A. Texas Real Estate License Act (TRELA) and the Texas Real Estate Commission (TREC)

1. The purpose of TRELA and TREC is to protect the public of the State of Texas.

2. TRELA is the law that governs all real estate licensees and sets the powers for the TREC.

B. Commission composition

1. Nine members—six brokers and three members of the general public

2. Appointed by the governor, with the advice and consent of the state senate, to staggered six-year terms

3. One broker designated by the governor as chairperson

C. Commission duties and powers

1. Make and enforce rules and regulations

2. Establish standards of conduct and ethics for licensees

3. **Administer and enforce license law and levy civil fines**

4. Select an administrator and employees to administer the law

5. Issue active and probationary licenses and collect money for licenses and renewals

6. Conduct investigations (within four years after the incident), hold hearings, and issue injunctions

7. Suspend or revoke a license, and place on probation or reprimand a licensee

8. Initiate a cease and desist action

9. Inspect and accredit real estate education programs

10. Promulgate contracts and addenda

11. Enforce the Texas Timeshare Act

D. TREC will not

1. Mediate or settle commission or other disputes between licensees or brokerage firms

2. Recommend individual licensees to the public

3. Send licensees to jail

II.   TREC REAL ESTATE ADVISORY COMMITTEES

A. Broker-Lawyer Committee

1. Functions

   a) Drafts, revises, and recommends contract forms intended for use by licensees.

   b) Does not publish, promulgate, or approve, the forms; only TREC may promulgate real estate contract forms

2. Makeup

   a) Consists of 13 members

   b) Six brokers appointed by the Commission

   c) Six lawyers appointed by the president of the State Bar of Texas

   d) One public member appointed by the governor

3. Members serve staggered six-year terms

   a) Terms for two brokers and two lawyers expire every two years.

   b) The public member's term expires every six years.

B. Education Standards Advisory Committee

1. Function

   a) This committee reviews and revises education curriculum standards, course content requirements, and instructor certification requirements for all Texas real estate core, Salesperson Apprentice Education (SAE), and Mandatory Continuing Education (MCE) courses.

2. Consists of 12 members

   a) Seven active licensees (salespeople or brokers)

   b) Must have at least five years' active real estate experience

   c) Four education members who are TREC-approved real estate instructors or owners of approved real estate schools

   d) One public member

   e) No set terms

III.   HANDLING OF COMPLAINTS—INVESTIGATIONS, HEARINGS AND APPEALS, AND PENALTIES

A. Investigations

1. The Commission may initiate investigations on its own or in response to a signed written complaint.

2. The Commission will give priority to the investigation of a complaint filed by a consumer or from an enforcement case resulting from the consumer complaint.

3. The Commission uses a risk-based approach to assign priorities and investigate complaints.

   a) Pursues those with the highest impact to the public first

4. **Under TRELA, the following felonies or misdemeanors are criminal offenses that are grounds for suspension, revocation, or denial of a license:**

   a) Failure to act in professional manner

      (1) Being negligent , incompetent, dishonest, or untrustworthy

      (2) Allowing or working with another to break license law

(3) Allowing an unlicensed employee to act as a licensee

(4) Failing to advise a buyer to get an abstract or title insurance policy

(5) Offering property for sale by means of a lottery

(6) Failing to provide copies of all signed documents to the signing parties

(7) Breaking fair housing laws

b) Misrepresenting or deceiving the public

(1) Failing to disclose a material fact or <u>latent defect</u>

(2) Misrepresenting or making false promises

(3) Using deceptive practices

(4) <u>Advertising</u> in any form that is misleading

- Failing to identify an advertisement as being from a licensed brokerage (doing business as [d/b/a]) or identifying the name of the broker of record or name of the designated broker

c) Guaranteeing or promising <u>future profits</u> from resale of real estate

d) Failing to properly disclose the following:

(1) The brokerage relationship and whom the broker or salesperson <u>represents</u>

(2) Acting as an undisclosed principal in the sale or purchase of real estate

e) When listing or attempting to list

(1) Failing to give a <u>definite termination</u> date in a listing contract

- Exception—property management agreement

(2) Offering to sell or lease without the consent of the owner

- Includes placing signs or advertising the property

(3) Advertising a listing that is not the brokerage firm or brokers

(4) Offering terms other than those authorized by the owner

- Includes sharing confidential information (PTM)

(5) Attempting to solicit a seller of an active listing to terminate and list with the soliciting broker

f) When handling trust funds

(1) Commingling or converting funds

(2) Disbursing trust funds before closing or termination

(3) Failing to properly account for all trust funds

(4) Failing to keep trust funds in a Texas bank or title company

g) Commissions

(1) Receiving compensation (commission or rebates) from a party to a transaction without consent of the other parties

(2) Paying commission to unlicensed persons

(3) Complete list can be found in Rules Sections 541.1(a)(1)–(15), Criminal Offense Guidelines

B. Hearings

1. If after investigation, the Commission determines it is appropriate to deny, suspend, or revoke a person's license or certificate, the licensee is entitled to a hearing conducted by the State Office of Administrative Hearings.

2. TREC has the power to subpoena witnesses and documents for the hearing and may file suit through the attorney general.

3. Failure to obey a court order may be punished by the court as contempt.

4. Appeals of the TREC decision may be made to a district court.

C. Penalties

1. The commissioners, after the hearing, may

   a) revoke a license,

   b) cancel a license, or

   c) suspend a license.

2. A principal broker whose license is suspended must

   a) notify all the firm's salespersons and parties to existing contracts, and

   b) remit the escrow or trust money (if held by the broker) in accordance with instructions of the contract principals.

3. A salesperson whose license is suspended must notify the principal broker.

4. TREC can issue administrative penalties for violations.

   a) The penalty may not exceed $5,000 per day for each violation.

   b) However, each day a violation continues, it may be considered a separate violation for purposes of imposing a penalty.

IV.   REAL ESTATE RECOVERY TRUST ACCOUNT

A. This account is maintained by TREC.

1. Funds in the account must total $1 million at minimum.

B. The purpose of the account is to reimburse consumers who suffer damages caused by real estate licensees, certificate holders, or their employees.

C. Brokerage firms must display the Consumer Information Form 1-1 in a prominent location in each location, notifying the public of the availability of the recovery fund.

D. The account is funded from license fees.

1. At time of application, the applicant pays $10 into the trust account.

2. If the amount in the trust account drops below $1 million, each licensee is assessed $10 or a pro rata share at the time of renewal to bring the trust account back up to $1.7 million.

E. Consumers must apply within two years of the cause of action or offense.

F. Recovery maximums are as follows:

1. $50,000 per transaction, regardless of the number of claimants

2. $100,000 total per licensee, regardless of the number of claims

G. Remedies against licensee if funds are used are as follows:

1. The Commission may revoke a license if the Commission makes a payment from the Real Estate Recovery Trust Account to satisfy all or part of a judgment against the licensee.

    a) TREC may issue a probationary license instead of revoking.

2. Renewal of a license or a certificate will be held until repayment of the full amount plus interest is paid.

UNIT 2

Licensing

(Test questions: Salesperson, 2; Broker, 4)

I.   ACTIVITIES REQUIRING A LICENSE/EXCEPTIONS/SCOPE OF PRACTICE

A. TREC licensing requirements

1. The three-prong test to determine whether a real estate license is required is activity or dealing in <u>real property</u> for <u>compensation</u> for <u>others</u>.

2. A real estate license is required for any person or business entity that for compensation does any of the following:

   a) Lists

   b) Leases

   c) Buys

   d) Exchanges

   e) Auctions

   f) Negotiates

   g) Sells

      (1) Remember, you need a license if you <u>LLBEANS</u> real property for others and are compensated.

3. In Texas, a person who acts as a real estate licensee without an active real estate license is guilty of a Class A misdemeanor.

   a) Punishable by a maximum <u>$4,000 fine</u> and/or up to <u>one year</u> in jail

4. Practicing without a license

   a) Punishable by a court, which may charge a penalty of <u>one to three times</u> the total money received

B. Obtaining a Texas salesperson or broker license

The Texas Real Estate Commission (TREC) recognizes two levels of responsibility for licensees, which are based on experience and additional education.

1. Salesperson license—no experience in real estate required

   a) Must be

      (1) at least 18 years old,

      (2) a U.S. citizen or legal alien,

      (3) a legal resident of Texas at time of filing, and

      (4) working under the supervision of a principal or sponsoring broker

   b) Complete required salesperson education of 12 semesters or 180 hours, which include

      (1) four semesters or 60 hours of principles of real estate; and

      (2) two semesters or 30 hours each of agency, contracts, contract forms and addenda, and real estate finance

    c) Submit a written application and required fee to TREC

       (1) Salesperson Sponsorship Form

          (a) Can be submitted before or after passing the exam; however, an active license cannot be issued without a sponsoring broker

       (2) Certifications showing completion of the required education

       (3) Fast Fingerprint Pass with fingerprinting done by either Morpho Trust or the test provider

    d) Receive the TREC letter of eligibility to take the license exam

       (1) Schedule to take the exam with the test provider; exam must be passed within one year of the date of filing the TREC application

    e) Satisfy TREC as to the honesty, trustworthiness, integrity, and competency of the applicant

       (1) Information on the application, submitting fingerprints, and passing the licensing exam is considered proof.

2. Broker's license—experience required

    a) Applicant must have a minimum of four years of active experience as a Texas licensee, in the 60 months (five years) preceding the application date.

    b) Applicant must complete required education of 60 semesters or 900 hours, which include the following:

       (1) At least 18 semesters or 270 hours of core courses, including two semesters or 30 hours in real estate brokerage

       (2) Remaining 42 semesters or 630 hours in core real estate courses or college credit from a bachelor's degree or higher and accepted by TREC

3. Applicant must pass the state broker's license exam.

4. After receiving the broker's license, the licensee is qualified to hire and supervise other licensees.

    a) If acting as a managing broker, will have additional duties to supervise licensees under, including

       (1) making sure all contract obligations are fully met,

       (2) meeting all compliance and regulatory requirements,

       (3) establishing office policy and compensation requirements; and

       (4) taking TREC's Broker Responsibility Course

C. Certificate of registration

1. A person who receives compensation for selling, buying, transferring, or leasing rights-of-way in connection with telecommunication, utility, railroad, or pipeline companies must have

    a) an active salesperson license **or**

b)   a certificate of registration from TREC.

    (1) Certificate of registration is good for two years.

    (2) No education or exam is required for a certification.

    (3) Certification can be revoked if TRELA or TREC rules are broken.

D. Other license issues

1. If TREC declines to issue a license,

    a)   it must immediately give written notice,

    b)   allow an appeal by the applicant, and

    c)   may issue a probationary license

        (1) Issued in instances where the licensee does not meet all the criteria for a full active license

2. Licensees with an inactive or expired license are prohibited from practicing real estate.

E. License examination

1. The license exam is administered by a testing service for TREC.

    a)   Per guidelines, any test-taker, Commission-approved education provider, or instructor may NOT do the following:

        (1) Attempt to obtain specific exam question or answers

        (2) Remove or attempt to remove questions or answers from the exam site

        (3) Provide or attempt to provide exam questions or answers to another person

2. The exam is composed of two portions: national and state.

    a)   The salesperson exam has 80 national questions and 30 state-specific questions.

    b)   The broker exam has 10 additional state-specific questions.

        (1) Both exams allow 150 minutes to complete the national portion and 90 minutes to complete the state-specific portion.

        (2) All test-takers must pass both portions of the exam.

            (a) Salespersons must pass with a 70% score.

            (b) Brokers must pass with a 75% score.

        (3) If failing one portion of the exam, the test-taker only needs to retake the failed portion.

        (4) Test-takers must have two forms of identification, which must match the TREC eligibility letter.

            (a) One must have a picture and be government issued, such as a driver's license or passport.

3. The test service is required to provide reasonable accommodations for any applicant with a verifiable disability. Test-takers needing such accommodations should contact the testing service.

F. License maintenance and renewal

1. Expiration and renewal

    a) All real estate licenses are good for two years and expire on the date shown on the face of the license certificate.

    (1) The expiration date is set from the date the license is issued.

    b) To renew a license, all licensees must complete continuing education.

    (1) Salesperson Apprentice Education (SAE) requirement for first renewal two years after receiving the initial license

2. A salesperson must provide TREC with evidence of completion of an additional six semesters or 90 hours for a cumulative total of 18 semesters or 270 hours pre- and post-license.

3. If the salesperson manages one or more licensees for a six-month period or longer, the Broker Responsibility Course is required as part of the 90 hours.

    a) Mandatory Continuing Education (MCE) requirements apply to all licensees after the first renewal.

    (1) Broker and salesperson licensees must complete a total of 15 hours in every two-year license renewal period.

    (a) The 15 hours must include six classroom hours of TREC-created courses, which include three hours of legal update and three hours of ethics update.

    (b) The balance of nine hours may be completed in any TREC-approved elective courses, which can be taken in a classroom or by distance learning.

4. If a licensed broker is also the broker of record (principal broker), designated broker, or a broker or salesperson acting as a delegated licensee, the six-hour Broker Responsibility Course is required. However, any licensee is allowed to take this course.

G. Professional ethics and conduct

1. All licensees must comply with the Canons of Professional Ethics and Conduct for real estate licensees, which are as follows:

    a) Fidelity: A licensee while acting as an agent as a fiduciary puts the principal's interest above all others, including the agents. All licensees are expected to deal fairly with all parties.

    b) Integrity: A licensee must be prudent and cautious to avoid all acts of misrepresentation.

    c) Competency: A licensee must be knowledgeable and informed and exercise judgment and skill. Competency is gained through education and experience.

    d) The Consumer Information Form 1-1 must be posted in a prominent location in each place of business the broker or inspector maintains. (See Recovery Trust Account.)

    e) Discriminatory practices: Licensees must obey all federal, state, and local fair housing laws and may not discriminate in any instance. Remember: FReSH CoRN (Family status, Race, Sex, Handicap, Color, Religion, and Nationality).

H. Transfer and inactive license status

1. Brokerage firms

   a) Principal brokers must have a fixed office and obtain a TREC branch office license for each additional brokerage office they maintain.

   b) If the brokerage firm changes addresses, the principal broker must apply to TREC for a new license within 10 days.

2. Assumed names

   a) Licensees and brokerage firms may operate under an assumed name—for example, a broker by the name of John Smith who conducts business under the name XYZ Reality.

   b) Licensee and firms operating under an assumed name must meet the following requirements:

      (1) Individual licensees and individual brokers (not brokerage firms)

         (a) Must file a certificate of assumed name with the county clerk in each county in which they conduct real estate

         (b) Must advise TREC of assumed name within 30 days after the assumed name or a different name is no longer used

3. Corporations and other business entities, such as a limited partnership or limited liability company

   a) Must register with TREC and identify the name of the designated broker

   b) Must file a certificate of assumed name with the secretary of state

   c) Must also file in the office of the county clerk of the county in which the registered office is located

4. TREC must be able to locate all licensees.

   a) Salespersons are tracked through their principal broker.

   b) The principal broker is required to keep the Commission informed of any changes of address.

   c) If a salesperson leaves a brokerage firm or is terminated, the following must occur:

      (1) The principal broker must return the salesperson's license to TREC immediately.

      (2) The salesperson must immediately notify the principal broker of intent to leave the firm.

      (3) When a salesperson's license is returned, it becomes inactive but may be reactivated upon submitting a new principal broker sponsorship application and the required fee.

         (a) The salesperson's license will become active under the new principal broker from the date the notice was mailed or delivered to TREC.

I. Exemptions to the license law

1. The following may complete a real estate transaction or complete certain real estate activities without a license :

   a) A person hired as a host or hostess at an open house

   b) A licensed auctioneer auctioning real estate

      (1) The host or hostess and auctioneer may not engage in any activity for which a license is required. Remember: LLBEANS

   c) An attorney licensed in Texas, with no requirement to be licensed to act as a broker

   d) An attorney-in-fact under a power of attorney

   e) A person under a court order , will, or trust (e.g., trustees , executors , or administrators)

   f) Public officials while engaged in official duties

   g) Trustees selling foreclosed properties at auction

   h) Onsite managers of an apartment complex

   i) Transactions involving only mineral or mining interests

   j) A new-home sales employee selling for a new homebuilder

Standards of Conduct

(Test questions: Salesperson, 7; Broker, 9)

I. PROFESSIONAL ETHICS AND CONDUCT

A. Commission Fees

    1. Typically, all fees are paid to the brokerage firm, which then splits the fees with all employed brokers and salespersons.

        a) Salespeople may receive compensation only from the principal broker who sponsored them.

            (1) Never from another broker or brokerage

        b) A salesperson may not pay a commission to another licensee, except with the written consent of the salesperson's principal broker.

    2. Brokers may not pay referral fees to unlicensed persons.

    3. Brokers may give merchandise gifts to unlicensed persons as long as the value does not exceed $50 retail value.

        a) Brokers cannot give cash in any amount.

        b) This rule does not apply to giving money to the principals to the transaction, even if they are unlicensed, because this is typically seen as a negotiation or renegotiation of the broker's fees.

    4. To file a court action to collect unpaid fees, brokers or salespeople must

        a) prove they were licensed at the time the fees were due, and

        b) have a written and signed listing or other agreement showing how the fees were to be paid and when they would be owed.

    5. Licensees who fail to advise buyers to obtain a title opinion of any abstract or a title insurance policy may not receive payment or recover any commission that the parties agreed to pay the brokerage.

II. UNAUTHORIZED PRACTICE OF LAW

A. Real estate brokers and salespeople may not offer legal advice, including advising consumer on the following:

    1. How to take title to real property

    2. The validity of any documents, including contracts and deeds

    3. The marketability of title to real property

B. Licensees may not draft any document that transfers or otherwise affects an interest in real property.

C. Licensees may complete a contract form for an interest in real property if

    1. the form was promulgated by TREC,

    2. it was prepared by an attorney licensed in Texas, or

    3. it was prepared by the property owner.

D. Penalties for violation include suspension and revocation of the real estate license.

III.   TRUST ACCOUNTS

A.   Overview

1.   Trust accounts are required anytime a real estate brokerage firm or broker is going to hold money that belongs to other people (e.g., earnest money).

2.   Trust accounts must follow specific rules established by statute and TREC and are subject to audit, at any time, by the Commission.

B.   Establishing brokerage accounts

1.   Brokerage firms and brokers typically have two types of accounts:

   a)   <u>Operations</u> used for running the firm

      (1)   Real estate commissions owed are paid from the brokerage's or broker's <u>operations account</u>.

   b)   <u>Trust accounts</u> are used to hold money (trust funds) for the benefit of others

      (1)   These accounts may not contain operating funds or any funds belonging to employed brokers or salespersons.

      (2)   Commissions must be removed from trust account within <u>30 days</u>.

      (3)   They may contain sufficient brokerage/broker funds to open and operate the account.

2.   <u>Salespersons</u> are not permitted to have trust accounts.

3.   Brokers and brokerages may use title companies to hold funds instead of having a trust account.

4.   Trust account rules governing brokers and brokerages are as follows:

   a)   Must use a <u>high level</u> of accuracy and care

   b)   Personally responsible for the funds in the trust account

   c)   Must have a recordkeeping system and retain all account records for <u>four years</u>

C.   Operating a trust account

1.   The broker is responsible for supervising the trust accounts.

2.   Brokers may authorize other persons to sign on the account.

3.   If an earnest money check is returned for <u>nonsufficient funds (NSF)</u>, the broker must immediately notify all parties to the transaction.

D.   Commingling/conversion of trust account funds

1.   <u>Commingling</u> is the improper mixing of operating account funds with trust account funds.

   a)   Not promptly removing earned commissions or fees from the trust account is an example of commingling.

2.   The illegal practice of <u>conversion</u> is the use of one party's funds for the benefit of another party.

   a)   A trust account may have a <u>zero balance</u> at times—this is not commingling or conversion. However, a negative balance in a trust account is conversion.

E. Handling trust or escrow accounts

1. Earnest money deposits

   a) Earnest money is typically deposited in a title company escrow account.

   b) Brokerages <u>may</u> hold earnest money in an identifiable trust/escrow account

   c) Earnest money must be deposited no later than the end of the <u>second business</u> day *after* the effective date of the contract.

2. If the licensee accepts the funds of another, those funds must be deposited into the brokerage trust or escrow account.

   a) Property management companies have individual trust or escrow accounts for their clients.

IV. BROKER RESPONSIBILITIES

A. Broker's responsibilities for salespersons/splitting fees

1. Brokers are responsible for all professional acts and conduct of their salespersons.

   a) Brokers are not required to directly supervise salespersons.

2. Complaints against a salesperson or a corporation are complaints against the sponsoring or designated broker.

3. Brokers may split fees as follows:

   a) With their own salespersons

   b) With resident brokers

   c) With nonresident brokers, as long as nonresident brokers do not conduct negotiations in Texas

B. Listing agreements

1. In any listing contract or buyer/tenant representation agreement, there must be a section that informs the parties that real estate commissions are negotiable.

2. It is legal for a broker to *rebate* a portion of the commission to the principal provided

   a) the payment is strictly a rebate and is not made for a real estate service, such as a referral.

   b) The rebate may be in any form:

   (1) Cash

   (2) Gift certificates

   (3) Appliances

   (4) Frequent flyer certificates

   (5) Other

3. Listings adopted by TREC must include a section explaining the availability of Texas coastal natural hazards information important to coastal residents.

4. A broker may not assign a listing agreement, buyer's representation agreement, or other personal service contract to another broker without written consent of the other party.

V.   ADVERTISING RULES

A. Disciplinary action may be taken against a licensee

1. who publishes any advertisement that misleads or is likely to deceive the public;

2. who tends to create a misleading impression; or

3. who fails to identify the name of the brokerage, broker of record, or designated broker.

B. Deceptive or misleading advertising includes, but is not limited to, the following:

1. Inaccurately advertising a material fact

2. Misrepresenting any property, terms, values, services, or policies

3. Failing to remove an advertisement about a listed property within a reasonable time after closing

4. Failing to clearly disclose the permitted uses of the property

C. All advertising must clearly and conspicuously contain the name of the broker, either a business entity or an individual.

1. The font of the business entity, broker of record, or designated broker must be no less than 50% of the largest font used in the advertisement.

2. Assumed names, if used, must be the name <u>registered</u> with the Commission.

3. Key: It should be relatively easy for a consumer to identify exactly which office and licensed broker are advertising.

UNIT

4

Agency/Brokerage

(Test Questions: Salesperson, 8; Broker, 10)

I.   AGENCY POSITIONS AND DISCLOSURE

A.   Disclosure of representation

1. Oral or written

2. At time of first contact in a proposed transaction

   a) With another party

   b) With a licensee representing another party

3. If the broker's representation changes, a new disclosure must be given.

   a) Includes changing from representation of only one party to an intermediary relationship

   b) Includes changing to an appointed license holder from an intermediary position

4. The brokerage must disclose to all parties in the proposed transaction if there are any relationship(s) between an associate of the brokerage and another party in the transaction. A relationship(s) is defined as a relative, close friend, or business associate.

B.   Information About Brokerage Services form

1. At the first substantive dialogue with a party concerning a specific piece of property

   a) The licensee must provide the mandatory written statement outlining the agency relationships allowed in brokerage services in Texas.

   b) Dual agency is not a choice in this form because it is no longer allowed.

2. The first substantive dialogue is "a meeting or written communication that involves a substantive discussion relating to specific real property."

3. The statutory wording of the mandatory written statement Information About Brokerage Services form that is approved by TREC for voluntary use.

   a) Any format is allowed as long as it contains the mandatory wording in at least 10-point type.

4. Exceptions

   a) Open house

   b) A party that is already represented by another licensee

   c) A meeting that takes place after a contract has been signed between the parties

   d) A residential lease of one year or less in which no sale is being considered

5. The Information About Brokerage Services form is an informational form.

   a) It is not a disclosure of agency.

   b) It is not a notice of an agency representation.

   c) It is not an addendum.

   d) It is not an amendment.

   e) It is not an agreement.

C. Intermediary brokerage

1. A broker acting as intermediary under Texas law

   a) Must have consent of each party in writing

   b) Must disclose any source of expected compensation to the broker

2. The intermediary

   a) must comply with the Texas Real Estate License Act (TRELA);

   b) must treat all parties honestly, fairly, and impartially;

   c) may not disclose that the seller will accept less than the asking price unless authorized in writing to do so by the owner;

   d) may not disclose that the buyer will pay a price greater than the price in the written offer unless authorized in writing to do so by the buyer; and

   e) may not disclose any confidential information or any information that a party specifically instructs the broker in writing not to disclose

      (1) Unless authorized in writing to disclose the information

      (2) Unless required to do so by the Texas Real Estate License Act or a court order

      (3) If the information materially relates to the condition of the property

3. If the parties consent in writing, the broker may appoint an associated license holder to each party to communicate with and carry out the instructions of the party.

   a) Unlike the intermediary, an appointed license holder may give advice and opinions.

   b) Even appointed license holders must not violate the intermediary/appointed license holder obligations

      (1) May not disclose that the seller will accept less than the asking price unless authorized in writing to do so by the owner

      (2) May not disclose that the buyer will pay a price greater than the price in the written offer unless authorized in writing to do so by the buyer

      (3) May not disclose any confidential information or any information that a party specifically instructs the broker in writing not to disclose

         ■ Unless authorized in writing to disclose the information

         ■ Unless required by the Texas Real Estate License Act or a court order

         ■ If the information materially relates to the condition of the property

4. A broker acting as an intermediary cannot be one of the appointed license holders.

   a) Any license holder in the brokerage who makes appointments for the broker cannot appoint self as one of the appointed license holders.

5. The broker may delegate the authority to appoint the associates to work with, carry out the instructions of, and give advice and opinions to the respective parties, but the broker remains as the impartial intermediary.

   a) If the broker delegates authority to appoint associated licensees to another licensee in the firm, the delegate making appointments may not delegate self as one of the appointed license holders and must remain impartial and act as the intermediary (i.e., impartial).

6. Associates must be appointed in writing to work with, communicate with, carry out the instructions of, and give advice and opinions to the respective parties.

   a) Associates not so appointed must remain impartial, even if they continue to work with two clients without written appointments.

7. A broker must agree to act as an intermediary in a transaction if the broker agrees to represent both parties in the same transaction because dual agency is not permitted in Texas.

   a) Dual agency is effectively prohibited by this section; TRELA Section 1101.561 states, "The duties of a license holder acting as an intermediary under this subchapter supersede the duties of a license holder established under any other law, including common law."

D. Mandatory disclosures

1. The seller, seller's agent, and buyer's agent must reveal all known material property defects to the buyer.

   a) A licensee, who withholds material factual information from a client, misstates, or lies to either the agent's client or another party to the transaction about material facts, may be guilty of misrepresentation or fraud.

2. A seller or an agent has no duty to release information related to whether a death occurred on the property if the death was due to

   a) natural causes,

   b) suicide, or

   c) an accident unrelated to the condition of the property.

3. Sellers or agents may have no statutory duty to disclose a death by murder on the property.

   a) They may incur a liability for such nondisclosure if a buyer alleges a violation under the Deceptive Trade Practices Act (DTPA).

   b) Death on the property resulting from the conditions of the property should be disclosed.

4. Disclosure regarding whether a previous or current occupant has or had HIV/AIDS is prohibited under TREC Rules.

   a) Federal fair housing law also prohibits such disclosures.

   b) TRELA states the following:

      (1) "Notwithstanding other law, a license holder is not required to inquire about, disclose, or release information relating to whether

         ■ a previous or current occupant of real property had, may have had, has, or may have AIDS, an HIV-related illness, or an HIV infection as defined by the Centers for Disease Control and Prevention of the United States Public Health Service; or

■ a death occurred on a property by natural causes, suicide, or accident unrelated to the condition of the property."

5. Information about the location of registered sex offenders does not have to be disclosed in relation to single-family homes, but neither is it prohibited.

6. Other required disclosures include the existence of an endangered species on property, if property is in a municipal utility district (MUD) or is coastal property.

7. A listing agent has a duty to present all offers to the client, unless otherwise specified in writing. Multiple offers should be presented simultaneously or as soon as possible after receipt of each offer.

8. An agent owes fiduciary duties to a client

   a) Obedience

   b) Loyalty

   c) Disclosure

   d) Confidentiality

   e) Accounting

   f) Reasonable skill and care

9. The *minimum services requirement* of the License Act dictates that a limited service broker

   a) Must inform the client if material information related to the transaction is received by the broker

   b) Must answer the client's questions and present any offer to or from the client

   c) May not instruct another broker to negotiate directly with the client

II.   ENFORCING COMPENSATION AGREEMENTS

A.   A person may not sue to collect compensation for an act as a broker or a salesperson that is performed in this state unless that person alleges and proves status, as follows:

1. As a license holder at the time the act was commenced

2. As an attorney licensed in Texas (TRELA Section 1101.005(1))

B.   A person in this state may not sue to recover a commission for the sale or purchase of real estate, unless

1. the promise or agreement on which the action is based, or a memorandum, is in writing, or

2. signed by the party against whom the action is brought or by a person authorized by that party to sign the document.

C. A license holder may not receive payment of or recover any commission agreed to be paid on the sale if, when an offer to purchase the real estate is signed, the licensee fails to

1. advise the buyer, in writing, to have the abstract covering the subject real estate examined by an attorney chosen by the buyer, or

2. provide a title insurance policy (usually by the seller) or obtain a title insurance policy.

   a) In addition to no entitlement to commission, the licensee who fails to give such written notice before closing is subject to potential loss of license by TREC.

   b) TREC contract forms, TAR contract forms, and TAR Buyer Representation Agreements already contain this advice.

      (1) Acceptable exception use contract forms as allowed by TREC Rules may not, and in most cases will not, contain the required language.

      (2) TREC has produced the optional form Notice to Prospective Buyer for a licensee to use, which also contains a required Utility District Notice.

III. BROKER-SALESPERSON RELATIONSHIPS; BROKER'S RESPONSIBILITY FOR ACTS OF SALESPERSON

A. A broker is responsible for the authorized acts of the broker's salespersons.

1. The broker is not required to supervise the salespersons directly.

B. The brokerage firm owns all contracts.

C. The sponsoring broker is responsible for all contracts.

1. Listings (employment)

2. Purchase agreements

IV. APPROPRIATE USE OF UNLICENSED ASSISTANTS

A. May perform certain tasks

1. Answering phone calls

2. Maintaining records

3. Handling correspondence

4. Scheduling appointments

5. Serving as hosts or hostesses at open houses

B. May not engage in any activity for which a license is required

Contracts

(Test questions: Salesperson, 7; Broker, 8)

I. TEXAS-PROMULGATED CONTRACT FORMS

A. Use of standard contract forms

1. When negotiating contracts binding the sale, exchange, option, lease, or rental of property,

   a) licensees must use only those contract forms promulgated or approved by the Texas Real Estate Commission (TREC) for that kind of transaction.

      (1) Promulgated means that the contracts are issued by TREC for mandatory use by license holders.

2. Exceptions

   a) Transaction in which the licensee is functioning solely as a principal, not an agent

   b) Transaction in which an agency of the U.S. government requires that a different form be used

   c) Transaction in which a form has been prepared by a principal to the transaction or by an attorney and required by a principal to the transaction

   d) Transaction for which no standard form exists and the licensee uses a form prepared by an attorney-at-law licensed in Texas and approved by the attorney for the particular kind of transactions involved or prepared by the Texas Real Estate Broker-Lawyer Committee and made available for trial use by TREC

3. Forms may be reproduced only from the following sources:

   a) Numbered copies obtained from TREC

   b) Printed copies made from copies obtained from TREC

   c) Legible photocopies made from such copies

   d) Computer-driven printers following mandatory guidelines

4. No changes may be made to TREC promulgated forms, except as follows:

   a) The business name or logo of a broker may appear at the top of a form outside the border.

   b) The broker's name may be inserted in any blank provided for that purpose.

5. Licensees may not add to or strike matter from forms, with the following exceptions:

   a) To add factual statements and business details desired by the principals

   b) To strike only such matter as is desired by the principals and as is necessary to conform the instrument to the intent of the parties (Rules Section 537.11(f)).

   c) Only if no other TREC-promulgated form exists for that purpose

6. It is not the practice of law as defined in this act for a real estate licensee to complete a contract form that is either

   a) TREC-promulgated, or

   b) Prepared by TREC and made available for trial use by licensees with TREC's consent.

B. Texas-promulgated contracts

1. One- to Four-Family Residential Contract (Resale)

2. Unimproved Property Contract

3. Farm and Ranch Contract

4. New Home Contract (Completed Construction)

5. New Home Contract (Incomplete Construction)

6. Residential Condominium Contract (Resale)

C. Selected Texas Addenda

1. Third Party Financing Addendum for Credit Approval

   a) To be used if the buyer is applying for a third-party loan to purchase property

   b) Used for conventional, Texas Veterans Housing Assistance Program Loan, FHA Insured, and VA Guaranteed Financing

   c) Time is of the essence (times and dates to be construed strictly as written in the addendum).

2. Seller Financing Addendum

   a) The buyer and seller can agree that the buyer will provide certain documentation to establish the buyer's creditworthiness or the seller can terminate the contract.

   b) The seller has seven days after receipt of the buyer's credit documentation to terminate the contract at the seller's sole discretion.

3. Addendum for Sale of Other Property by Buyer

   a) The addendum provides a contingency for the buyer

      (1) to terminate the contract without default, or

      (2) to continue in the contract by removing the contingency and depositing additional earnest money in case the buyer cannot sell a named property owned by the buyer.

   b) The seller may continue to show property, and if a subsequent offer from a second buyer is accepted by the seller,

      (1) the seller can require the first buyer to waive the contingency and put up additional earnest money, or

      (2) the seller can require the first buyer to terminate the first contract and take back the earnest money.

      (3) If the first buyer elects to terminate, the second buyer's contract (which should have an Addendum for "Back-Up" Contract attached) will become the primary contract.

   c) Time is of the essence (times and dates to be construed strictly as written in the addendum).

4. Addendum for "Back-Up" Contract

   a) This addendum is to be used as an addendum to a second buyer's offer when the seller is already under contract with a first buyer.

      b) It provides a contingency on its effectiveness to be based on the termination of the first buyer's contract.

      c) Neither party is required to perform during the contingency period.

          (1) Although earnest money and any option fee must be paid if required by the contract.

      d) Time is of the essence (times and dates to be construed strictly as written in the addendum).

  5. Addendum for Coastal Area Property—Natural Resources Code

      a) The owner of the property may gain or lose portions of the tract because of changes in the boundary of "state-owned tidally influenced submerged lands."

      b) State law prohibits the use, encumbrance, construction, or placing of any structure in, on, or over state-owned submerged lands.

  6. Addendum for Property Located Seaward of the Gulf Intracoastal Waterway—Natural Resources Code

      a) Provides notice that if property is in close proximity to a beach fronting the Gulf of Mexico,

          (1) the public has an easement to or over the area of any public beach

      b) States that state law prohibits any obstruction to the public easement

          (1) Structures erected on or over the easement are subject to a lawsuit to remove them

  7. Addendum for Reservation of Oil, Gas, and Other Minerals

      a) Provides to the seller to reserve mineral rights in percentage or in whole

      b) Addresses existing leases with entities that have ingress and egress rights

D. Selected notices, amendments, and other forms (not addenda)

  1. Seller's Temporary Residential Lease

      a) Used when the seller retains possession of the property for not more than 90 days after closing

  2. Buyer's Temporary Residential Lease

      a) Used when the buyer takes possession of the property not more than 90 days prior to closing

  3. Notice of Buyer's Termination of Contract

      a) Used by a broker when the buyer wishes to notify the seller that the contract is terminated

      b) Six different contractual rights to terminate addressed in the notice

  4. Amendment to Contract

      a) Used to modify an existing contract and/or addendum to a contract

      b) Contains nine contract subject areas to amend or modify

          (1) Includes one labeled "Other Modifications"

5. Notice to Prospective Buyer

     a) Used when TREC-promulgated contract forms are not being used under the *exceptions* rule, and/or

     b) Used when the buyer's agent has not used a Buyer Representation Agreement that already contains these notices

6. Texas Real Estate Consumer Notice Concerning Hazards or Deficiencies

     a) Used to increase buyer awareness of hazards and reduce broker liability

7. Seller's Disclosure of Property Condition

     a) Contains only the minimum requirements of the Texas Property Code Section 5.008

     b) Many brokers use their own versions or TAR versions with many additional items of disclosure than what is required by the Texas Property Code Section 5.008.

8. Information About Brokerage Services

     a) Used to give the statutorily required written statement concerning forms of agency or non-agency relationships lawfully provided to consumers by real estate licensees

     b) Format approved but optional

     c) Wording contained within the form required by state law even if the licensee uses a different form

     d) Written statement must be in at least 10-point type

     e) Not an addendum and should not be attached to or made a part of the offer/contract

     f) Statute does not require anyone to sign this document

         (1) Good business practice to get it signed as evidence it was presented

II. STATUTE OF FRAUDS

A. Agreement in writing and signed

1. According to the statute of frauds

     a) A promise or agreement for the sale of real property, or for the lease of real property for more than one year, is not enforceable unless

         (1) the agreement is in writing and signed by the person to be charged with the agreement or by someone lawfully authorized to sign for that person, and

         (2) both spouses sign agreements to release community property and homestead rights.

2. Debt agreements and contracts for the transfer of real estate, but not leases of 12 months or less, are included.

3. Oral contracts for the sale of real estate or for the lease of real estate for more than one year are not illegal.

     a) These oral contracts are simply unenforceable by law.

B. Purpose of the statute of frauds

    1. Prevent fraud by someone seeking the enforcement of a contract that was never made

    2. Disallow fraudulent oral evidence of a fictitious contract

    3. Protect spouses' rights in property

III. REMEDIES FOR BREACH OF CONTRACT/DEFAULT REPLACEMENT NOTICE CONTAINED IN TREC-PROMULGATED CONTRACT FORMS

A. Seller's remedies for buyer's default

    1. Enforce specific performance (court action to force breaching party to perform)

    2. Seek such other relief as provided by law (e.g., suit for damages, injunction, etc.)

    3. Terminate the contract and receive earnest money as liquidated damages

        a) This would release both parties from contract.

B. Buyer's remedies for seller's default

    1. If, due to factors beyond the seller's control, the Commitment and Exception documents are not delivered within the time required,

        a) the buyer may terminate this contract and the earnest money will be refunded to the buyer.

    2. If the seller fails to furnish the existing survey or affidavit within the prescribed time,

        a) the buyer shall obtain a new survey at seller's expense no later than three days before the closing date.

    3. If the seller fails to complete any agreed repairs and treatments before the closing date, the buyer may

        a) exercise remedies under Paragraph 15, or

        b) extend the closing date up to five days if necessary for seller to complete the repairs and treatments.

    4. If the seller fails to comply with the contract for any other reason, the buyer may

        a) enforce specific performance, seek such other relief as may be provided by law, or both; or

        b) terminate this contract and receive the earnest money, thereby releasing both parties from the contract.

C. Statute of limitations

    1. Action to bring suit or enforce rights must be brought

        a) within four years for a written contract, or

        b) within two years for an oral contract.

IV.   TERMINATION OPTION

A.   A termination option allows a buyer, for a nominal fee, the unrestricted right to terminate a contract based on accepted terms.

1. Time is of the essence with this option.

2. The buyer pays an option fee directly to the seller within three days after the effective date of the contract for this right.

3. Earnest money, unlike the option fee, is deposited by the buyer with the escrow agent **by the end of the second business day after the effective date or/and as directed in the contract**

4. According to TREC contract forms, earnest money is never given to the seller's agent but is deposited by the buyer.

V.   SELLER'S DISCLOSURE OF PROPERTY CONDITION FORM

A.   The seller of a single residential dwelling unit must complete and sign a Seller's Disclosure of Property Condition form.

1. The 11 exceptions to the requirements in this section that apply to a transfer are as follows:

    a) Pursuant to a court order or foreclosure sale

    b) By a trustee in bankruptcy

    c) To a mortgagee by a mortgagor or successor in interest or to a beneficiary of a deed of trust by a trustor or successor in interest

    d) By a mortgagee or a beneficiary under a deed of trust who

        (1) has acquired the real property at a sale conducted pursuant to a power of sale under a deed of trust or a sale pursuant to a court ordered foreclosure, or

        (2) has acquired the real property by a deed in lieu of foreclosure

    e) By a fiduciary in the course of the administration of a decedent's estate, guardianship, conservatorship, or trust

    f) From one co-owner to one or more other co-owners

    g) Made to a spouse or to a person or persons in the lineal line of consanguinity of one or more of the transferors

    h) Between spouses resulting from a decree of dissolution of marriage or a decree of legal separation or from a property settlement agreement incidental to such a decree

    i) To or from any governmental entity

    j) Of a new residence of not more than one dwelling unit which has not previously been occupied for residential purposes

    k) Of real property where the value of any dwelling does not exceed 5% of the value of the property

2. If the Seller's Disclosure of Property Condition form is required and not provided on or before the effective date of an executory contract binding the purchaser to purchase the property,

    a) the buyer may terminate the contract within seven days after receiving the notice or before closing, whichever is earlier; or

    b) if the disclosure form is not provided, the buyer may terminate the contract at any time before closing, and the earnest money will be returned.

6
UNIT

Special Topics

(Test questions: Salesperson, 4; Broker, 6)

I.   SEPARATE AND COMMUNITY PROPERTY

A.   Separate and community property

1.   State laws determine the way real and personal property, along with other assets, will be handled in case of death or divorce of the married owners.

B.   Separate property

1.   Separate property is

a)   real property acquired before marriage; or

b)   property acquired during marriage by gift, devise, descent, personal injury lawsuit, or by written contract with the spouse.

2.   All separate property, except the homestead, may be mortgaged or conveyed by the owning spouse without the consent of the other.

C.   Community property

1.   Community property is property acquired by either spouse during marriage that is not separate property.

a)   Income from separate property is considered community property unless there is a signed agreement between the spouses.

2.   All community property (and all homesteads) may be mortgaged or conveyed only with the signed consent of both spouses.

a)   This is known as the "one to buy, two to sell" rule.

II.   HOMESTEAD RIGHTS

A.   Homestead defined

1.   A statutory life estate that is owned and occupied as the primary residence

2.   Applies to single or married homeowners

a)   If the owners are married, the homestead rights are inheritable by the surviving spouse and minor children.

B.   Protections under the law

1.   Homeowners are protected from the forced sale of their residence by unpaid general creditors, such as credit card companies.

2.   Spouses are protected by the requirement that both spouses sign conveyances and mortgages.

3.   If allowed by zoning, a business may be run from the homestead.

4.   Proceeds from the sale of a homestead may be protected for up to six months.

5.   Homesteads may be terminated only through death, alienation, or abandonment.

C.   Requirements to claim homestead

1.   The property must be owned and occupied as the primary residence by the head of a family or a single person.

2. No filing is required—ownership and occupancy of a property as the principal place of residence automatically create the homestead.

3. To receive a homestead tax exemption to reduce property taxes, the owner must apply for the exemption with the county where the property is located.

4. Personal property may also be protected under homestead laws.

   a) For a maximum of $60,000 when owned by a family

   b) For a maximum of $30,000 for a single person

D. Homestead acreage limitations

1. Rural primary residence must be

   a) on a maximum of 200 acres for a family, or

   b) on a maximum of 100 acres for a single person.

2. Urban primary residence must be

   a) on a maximum of 10 acres (contiguous tract of land) for a family or a single person.

3. There are no limitations on the value of the homestead.

4. Homesteads don't protect the owner from all creditors and may be foreclosed by certain lienholders if the owner is in default or delinquent.

III. DECEPTIVE TRADE PRACTICES ACT (DTPA)

A. The purpose of the law

1. To protect consumers from false, misleading, and deceptive business practices

2. To provide procedures for compensation if the consumers can prove they were a victim

   a) Applies to any business, including those from outside of Texas, that sells to Texas consumers

B. Application to real estate licensees

1. The licensee is responsible for accurate representations and disclosure of all material facts, even if the contract specifies "as is."

2. Claims that involve providing advice, judgment, opinion, or similar professional skills, such as preparing a CMA, are excluded.

3. Licensees may still be charged if they

   a) misrepresent or fail to disclose a material fact; or

   b) make statements not characterized as advice, judgment, or opinion.

4. Puffing is making a statement anyone should understand as an exaggeration (e.g., "This is the best view in the world").

   a) This is typically not considered a violation or misrepresentation in other states.

   b) It will not be allowed as a defense under the law.

    c) An unthinking consumer may take a statement as fact, given the status of the licensee as a "professional with more knowledge."

C. Waivers

    1. Most waivers and disclaimers are void under DTPA.

    2. In order for a waiver to be effective, it must

        a) be conspicuous, in boldface, and at least 10-point type in size;

        b) be identified by the heading Waiver of Consumer Rights; and

        c) use the language prescribed by the law.

    3. This type of waiver is not typically used in real estate practices because all real estate professionals are obligated to advise all consumers to seek legal counsel.

D. Claims and damages

    1. Recovery may include economic damages plus an amount not to exceed treble (three times) the economic damages.

    2. Damages for mental anguish may be included if the conduct of the defendant was committed knowingly or with intention.

E. Statute of limitations

    1. A suit brought for a violation of the Deceptive Trade Practices Act must commence within two years from the date a buyer discovered or should reasonably have discovered the deceptive act.

IV. WILLS AND ESTATES

A. Passage of title to community property

    1. Upon the intestate death of one of the spouses in a marriage

        a) The community property estate of the deceased spouse passes to the surviving spouse if

            (1) no child or other descendant of the deceased spouse survives the deceased spouse, or

            (2) all surviving children and descendants of the deceased spouse are also children or descendants of the surviving spouse.

    2. If a child or other descendant of the deceased spouse is not a child or descendant of the surviving spouse,

        a) the child or other descendant and the surviving spouse split the community property 50/50.

V. LANDLORD-TENANT ISSUES

A. Security deposit

    1. Deposits must be returned or accounted for on or before the 30th day after the tenant surrenders the residential premises (60 days for commercial leases).

    2. All or part of the deposit may be retained if

        a) the tenant leaves no forwarding address or

        b) money is owed and not disputed by the tenant.

3. Deposits may not be used by the tenant to pay for the last month's rent.

    a) May be applied to actual damages done by the tenant

B. Landlord's lien

1. Landlords may file a lien for unpaid rent that attaches to tenants' personal property in the residence or storage.

2. A landlord may only collect a charge for removing or storing personal property if authorized to do so in the written lease.

3. A landlord must make an effort to notify a tenant 30 days before selling or disposing of the tenant's personal property (60 days in a commercial lease).

C. Assignment/sublease

1. Unless otherwise stated in the lease, a tenant may not assign or sublease without the landlord's written consent.

D. Security devices for residential rental dwellings

1. The landlord must rekey locks at each tenant turnover.

    a) The time frame is from the time the old tenant moves out but no later than seven days after the new tenant moves in.

2. Tenants must have the permission of the landlord to install new locks and must give a copy of the key to the landlord.

VI. FORECLOSURE SALE

A. Redemption periods

1. Most states have an equitable and statutory redemption period for loans foreclosed on real property.

    a) The equitable redemption period is the period before the sale when a borrower may stop the foreclosure by paying all back payments and fees.

        (1) In Texas, the debtor must have at least 20 days to cure the default before the lender can accelerate the note and set a foreclosure sale date.

2. The statutory redemption period comes after the foreclosure sale. During this period, the borrower must pay off the full principal plus all interest and fees to retain title.

    a) Texas has no statutory redemption for deed of trust.

    b) There is a statutory redemption period for property tax liens, which is two years for a homestead and six months for nonhomestead properties.

    c) There is a 180-day statutory redemption period for homeowners association liens (HOA lien).

B. Demand notice and intent to accelerate

1. Borrowers in default must be given a demand for payment notice, which allows them 20 days to bring payments current (equitable redemption).

2. If the loan is not redeemed, written notice of the sale must be given to the borrower at least 21 days before the foreclosure sale date.

3. Notice of the foreclosure sale must include the following:

    a) Posting at the door of the courthouse in the county where the property is located and the sale is to be conducted

    b) Filing it at the office of the county clerk

    c) Sending it by certified mail to each debtor obligated to pay the debt

C. Foreclosure sale

1. The sale is held by the trustee, between 10 am and 4 pm on the first Tuesday of the month at the county courthouse.

2. The property is sold to the highest bidder, who is often the lender, at the public sale. The winning bidder receives a sheriff's deed or sheriff's certificate of sale.

3. Proceeds from a foreclosure sale in excess of the mortgage indebtedness belong to the defaulting borrower.

4. Insufficient proceeds might result in a deficiency judgment. Texas law requires the lender to file for the judgment within two years after the foreclosure sale.

D. Short sale

1. A short sale occurs when a borrower is in default and instead of foreclosing, the lender allows the sale of the property.

2. These sales occur when the market value is less than the loan amount but the lender realizes a cost saving by not foreclosing.

3. In Texas, the TREC-promulgated Short Sale Addendum must be attached to the sale contract for this type of sale.

E. Recording

1. In Texas, real property deeds may not be recorded unless the deed is signed or sworn to by the grantor in front of a witness, usually a notary.

VII. MECHANICS' LIENS/MATERIALMEN'S LIENS

A. Mechanics' and materialmen's liens

1. Mechanic's lien basics

    a) A mechanic's lien is a specific, statutory lien that gives security to contractors, subcontractors, and others who provide services or materials, and can be foreclosed if not paid.

    b) In Texas, if property owners sign a mechanic's lien contract, they agree to allow the lien to be placed for nonpayment.

B. Texas mechanic's/materialman's lien requirements

1. Lien rights attach from when the first labor and/or material is furnished.

2. Contractors or subcontractors must have worked under a contract with the owner. If the contract is an expressed oral or an implied contract, the contractor or other party seeking payment will have to file an affidavit claiming a mechanic's lien.

3. If the property is a homestead, both spouses must sign the contract.

4. Contractors must furnish a final bills paid affidavit to the property owners upon receipt of the final payment.

5. Property owners may protect their property by requesting a lien waiver, which will not allow liens to be recorded.

6. A lien satisfaction is used to release a recorded lien.

VIII. VETERANS LAND BOARD

A. The Texas Veterans Land Board has three loan programs used to assist Texas veterans in either purchasing a primary residence or land or making home improvements.

1. The Veterans Housing Assistance Program makes available money to purchase a primary residence.

   a) The maximum loan under this program is capped at $325,000. However, there is no minimum or maximum sales price restrictions.

2. The Veterans Land Program originates loans for eligible Texas veterans to buy a minimum of one acre and finance a 95% loan of up to $80,000 over a 30-year term.

3. The Veterans Home Improvement Program is for eligible Texas veterans to make improvements to their current principal residence.

   a) This program is capped at $25,000 for a term of 20 years and does not require a down payment.

IX. HOMEOWNERS ASSOCIATIONS (HOA)

1. A homeowners association lien is enforceable against a homestead.

2. There is a 180-day statutory period of redemption when a property is foreclosed on for non-payment of HOA dues.

3. There are three TREC forms pertaining to HOAs:

   a) Addendum for Property Subject to Mandatory Membership in a Property Owners Association

   b) Subdivision Information, Including Resale Certificate For Property Subject to Mandatory Membership in a Property Owners' Association

   c) Condominium Resale Certificate

UNIT

7

Texas-Specific True/ False Questions

The state portion of the Real Estate License Exam comprises 40 scored questions for salespersons and 50 scored questions for brokers. These true/false questions are organized by the following topics:

- Commission Duties and Powers
- Licensing
- Standards of Conduct
- Agency/Brokerage
- Contracts
- Special Topics

I.   COMMISSION DUTIES AND POWERS

(Test questions: Salesperson, 2; Broker, 3)

1.	The Real Estate Commission must investigate every complaint against a licensee.	F Only signed written complaints are investigated.
2.	TREC has the power to make laws, rules, and regulations.	F TREC has the power to make rules and regulations. Laws are made by the state legislature.
3.	Once a complaint is ruled on by TREC, no other action can take place.	F A ruling by TREC may be appealed to a district court.
4.	TREC is authorized to settle commission disputes.	F TREC may not mediate disputes between brokers or salespeople.
5.	TREC is authorized to subpoena documentation or and witnesses.	T
6.	A real estate licensee may legally fill in contract forms that have been promulgated by the Commission.	T
7.	The Real Estate Broker-Lawyer Committee has the power to promulgate forms.	F The Real Estate Broker-Lawyer Committee drafts and revises contract forms. TREC promulgates forms.
8.	TREC approves and promulgates contract forms.	T
9.	The Texas Real Estate Commission consists of three brokers and six general members.	F TREC is composed of nine members, three general members and six brokers.
10.	A consumer's action to recover funds from the trust account must be taken within two years of the cause of action.	T
11.	Each applicant pays a fee of $100 at the time of application to the trust account.	F A $10 fee is paid to the trust account at the time of application and all renewals.
12.	The maximum amount to be paid from the trust account per violation is $50,000.	F The maximum is $50,000 per transaction, regardless of the number of violations, and $100,000 per licensee.
13.	Licensees may use forms prepared by an attorney licensed in Texas or by the property owner.	T
14.	The primary purpose of the Texas Real Estate License Act is to protect consumers.	T

15. A person who acts as a licensee without a license is guilty of a Class B misdemeanor.

F A person who acts as a licensee without a license is guilty of a Class C misdemeanor.

16. Real estate licensees may prepare a legal document if one does *NOT* already exist.

F Real estate licensees may never prepare legal documents for real estate transactions.

17. The Real Estate Commission's discipline of licensees may include a fine, license suspension, or license revocation.

T

18. The Real Estate Commission will investigate a purchaser's complaint regarding the failure of a licensee to disclose material fact that was known only by the seller.

F The licensee must also have known of the undisclosed material fact.

19. Brokers are responsible for their actions and the actions of the salesperson they sponsor in real estate.

T

20. The Broker-Lawyer Committee is made up ofmembers.

F There are a total ofmembers, six brokers, six attorneys, and one general person.

21. Licensees who have had their license suspended must notify their broker withindays.

F The broker must be notified immediately.

22. TREC appoints all the members of the Broker-Lawyer Committee.

F Only the six brokers are appointed by TREC. The six attorneys are appointed by the president of the State Bar of Texas and the general member is appointed by the governor.

23. One broker on the Commission is designated as chairperson.

T

24. TREC's administrative penalties cannot exceed $4,000 per day unless the licensee has a history of previous violations.

F Administrative penalties cannot exceed $5,000 per day unless the licensee has a history of previous violations.

25. The brokerage firm must maintain records of deposits to and withdrawals from a trust account for seven years.

F Four years

II.   LICENSING

(Test questions: Salesperson, 2; Broker, 4)

1.	TRELA does *NOT* apply to an attorney licensed in this state.	T
2.	Licensees may perform a CMA, a BPO, or an appraisal for the client of the broker.	F Real estate licensees are not allowed to perform an appraisal unless they are also a certified appraiser.
3.	Apartment locators and onsite apartment managers must obtain a real estate license and be under an active licensed broker.	F Apartment locators must be licensed; however, onsite apartment managers do not need to be licensed.
4.	A real estate license is *NOT* needed to sell or lease mineral rights.	T
5.	A Texas real estate broker may share part of the commission with a foreign broker.	T
6.	An employee of a business entity that buys property for the corporation is exempt from licensing requirements.	T
7.	One tenant can help find another tenant for the landlord and receive half of a month's rent discount.	F To receive a fee for assisting another to locate property for sale or rent is under the scope of practicing real estate.
8.	A licensed auctioneer, while conducting the sale of real estate by auction, does *NOT* have to hold a real estate license if the auctioneer does not perform another act of a broker or salesperson.	T
9.	Only licensees may host an open house.	F The host or hostess is not required to have a real estate license as long as the unlicensed person does not engage in activities that would require a real estate license.
10.	All real estate teams must have a sponsoring broker.	T
11.	Unless a business entity holds a license, it may *NOT* act as a broker.	T
12.	An apprentice inspector must perform at *LEAST* 20 inspections under the direct supervision of a professional inspector before becoming eligible for the inspector exam.	F The inspector apprentice must perform 25 inspections.
13.	A foreign broker is any broker outside of Texas.	T

14. A real estate license is *NOT* needed in dealing in options on real estate for another person for a fee.

   F A real estate license is needed when dealing in options on real estate, including buying, selling, or offering to buy or sell options on real estate for another person for a fee.

15. Real estate brokers are responsible to the public and to TREC for the professional actions of the salespeople they sponsor.

   T

16. A salesperson applicant must achieve at *LEAST* a 70% score on both the national and state portions of the licensing exam.

   T

17. A real estate applicant must be 21 years of age at time of application.

   F A real estate applicant must be 18 years of age at time of application.

18. To be eligible to apply for a salesperson's license, a person must complete 180 classroom hours of education as required by the TRELA.

   T

19. The Commission may issue a probationary license.

   T

20. TREC regards completing the required licensing courses and passing the licensing exam as evidence of a person's competency to engage in real estate brokerage.

   F Competency is established solely by passing the licensing exam.

21. The licensing exam must be of sufficient scope to determine whether a person is competent to act as a broker or salesperson in a manner that will protect the public.

   T

22. Applicants have six months to pass the exam once the application has been received.

   F Applicants have one year from the date of application to pass the exam.

23. A salesperson must be active two of the last five years to be eligible for a broker's exam.

   F A salesperson must be active four of the last five years to be eligible for a broker's exam.

24. Brokers must receive 15 hours of continuing education every year.

   F Brokers must receive 15 hours of continuing education every two years.

25. The education requirement for obtaining a salesperson's license is completion of six semester hours as required by the TRELA.

   F The education requirement for obtaining a salesperson's license is completion of 12 semester hours (180 classroom hours).

26. All applicants for a salesperson or broker license must provide fingerprints.

   T

27. Applicants must be a Texas resident for at *LEAST* three months prior to making application.

   F At the time of application, the applicant must be a resident of Texas.

28. SAE is an acronym for Salesperson Annual Education.

F   The acronym SAE is Salesperson Apprentice Education.

29. The salesperson must show 60 hours of SAE during the first two years of licensure.

F   The salesperson must complete 90 hours of SAE during the first two years of licensure.

30. After satisfying the SAE requirement, all licensees must take the TREC Legal and Ethics Update course every two years regardless of any other education requirement.

T

31. Once the sponsorship form and fee has been paid, a new licensee may begin practicing real estate.

F   Once the sponsoring broker has received the active license of a new salesperson, the salesperson may begin to practice real estate.

32. If the broker of record dies, the brokerage has 24 hours to name the new sponsoring broker before the salespersons' licenses become inactive.

F   If the broker of record dies, all representation ceases and the licensees must find another broker, fill out the broker sponsorship, and pay the $20 fee to be able to practice real estate.

33. The broker who terminates a licensee must return the salesperson's license to TREC immediately.

T

34. An inactive licensee returning to active status must complete 30 hours of continuing education during the two-year period preceding the application for active status.

F   An inactive licensee returning to active status must complete 15 hours of continuing education during the two-year period preceding the application for active status.

35. A nonprogrammable, pocket-size calculator without an alphabetic keyboard or communication capabilities is permitted at the examination site.

T

36. TREC may decline to issue a license and give no notice as to the cause of the decision.

F   If the Commission declines to issue a license, it must immediately give written notice and allow an appeal.

37. The new salesperson is prohibited from practicing real estate for another person for a fee, until the license has been received by the broker.

T

38. All licenses expire on the date the exam was passed.

F   All licenses expire on the date shown on the face of the license certificate.

39. A broker applicant must take the Broker Responsibility Course as an MCE requirement.

    F A broker applicant must take the 30-hour Real Estate Brokerage Course as part of the 900 licensing hours.

40. When taking the exam, attendees are allowed a sheet of paper to write down notes and take it with them when they leave.

    F If asked, a sheet of paper will be supplied when taking the exam; however, the sheet must be surrendered to the testing center.

41. An individual may hold an inactive salesperson license and an active broker license at the same time.

    F An individual may hold either a salesperson's or a broker's license, but not both at the same time.

42. The licensee has until the sixth month after expiration to renew the license.

    T

43. A broker who manages or oversees one or more licensees for a period of six months or longer must take the six-hour Broker Responsibility Course once.

    F A broker who manages or oversees one or more licensees for a period of six months or longer must take the six-hour Broker Responsibility Course for each active renewal period.

44. An application is known to be "timely filed" if it is received on or before the expiration date of the license.

    T

45. At the completion of the salesperson's first two-year renewal, the licensee will have a minimum of 280 classroom hours of education.

    F At the completion of the salesperson's first two-year renewal, the licensee will have a minimum of 270 classroom hours of education; 180 from the pre-licensing education and 90 from SAE.

III. STANDARDS OF CONDUCT

(Test questions: Salesperson, 7; Broker, 9)

1. If a broker moves from the address designated on the broker's license, the broker must apply for a new license for each new location within 30 days.

    F Within 10 days after a move, brokers must apply for a new license for each new location.

2. Brokers are responsible for the conduct of their salespersons and are required to directly supervise the salesperson's professional acts.

    F Brokers are responsible for the conduct of their salespersons but are not required to directly supervise the salesperson.

3. A listing contract form adopted by TREC must include a provision inform-ing the parties to the contract that real estate commissions are negotiable.

    T

4. A broker who maintains a trust must keep a record of all account deposits and withdrawals for a period of seven years.

    F The trust account docu-ments must be maintained for no less than four years for TREC and no less than seven years for the IRS.

5. A real estate broker or salesperson has a special obligation to exercise integrity in the discharge of the licensee's responsibilities.

    T

6. Licensees need *NOT* disclose their license status when selling property for a business entity unless they own more than 50% of the entity.

    F Licensees must disclose their license status when selling property for a busi-ness entity when they own 10% or more of the entity.

7. Salespeople may receive a referral fee from the other broker.

    F Salespeople may only receive commissions from their sponsoring broker.

8. Depositing money from the landlord client in the broker's personal account is known as conversion.

    F Depositing money from the landlord client in the broker's personal account is known as commingling.

9. Licensees may have their license revoked or suspended if they fail to make good on a bad check to the Commission.

    T

10. Licensees may place a For Sale sign on a vacant lot next to their own prop-erty without the consent of the property owner so that they may capture buyers.

    F A licensee may not place a For Sale sign on a property without the written consent of the owner or owner's agent.

11. All parties in a transaction have the right to receive all documents that have their signature or initials on the documents.

    T

12. Under the Canons of Professional Ethics and Conduct, fidelity provides that a real estate broker or salesperson, while acting as an agent for another, is a fiduciary. This demands that the primary duty of the real estate agent is to represent the interests of the seller, and the agent's position, in this respect, should be clear to all parties concerned in a real estate transaction.

    F The primary duty of the real estate agent is to represent the interests of the client. The agent's position, in this respect, should be clear to all parties concerned in a real estate transaction.

13. Displaying the Consumer Information Form 1-1 is evidence of nondiscriminatory practice.

    F TRELA requires brokers to display the Consumer Information Form 1-1 as a notification to the public of the availability of the recovery fund. Failure to display the HUD Equal Housing Opportunity Housing poster is considered by HUD to be evidence of discrimination.

14. The listing office is *NOT* obligated to disclose it is the agent for the seller because the sign and advertising states the listing is held with the brokerage.

    F It is grounds for suspension or revocation of a license to not disclose at first contact the representation between the brokerage and the seller.

15. Property management agreements are *NOT* bound to the same requirements of other representation agreements in regards to a definite termination date.

    T

16. A licensee may approach a seller directly if the listing office is unavailable.

    F It is permitted to negotiate a transaction directly with a seller who is under an exclusive agency agreement with another brokerage if the listing office is unavailable.

17. It is permissible for the broker to require the principals in a transaction to designate the broker as their escrow agent.

    F The broker may never require or demand to be the escrow agent in the transaction.

18. The broker may prepare a document to disclose the presence of a lien on the property a buyer is interested in purchasing.

    F It is illegal for any licensee to draw or prepare documents that define the legal rights.

19. As a marketing tool, licensees may pay for services on behalf of the principal—for example, an inspection, a home warranty, or legal advice.	**F** While it is permissible to pay for an inspection or home warranty with full disclosure to all parties, it is illegal to select or pay for legal counsel for either party in the transaction.
20. Licensees may use any contractual form when selling or purchasing real estate for themselves.	**T**
21. Guaranteeing that a property will turn a profit is permissible for investor clients.	**F** Guaranteeing that a property will turn a profit is grounds for revocation or suspension of a real estate license.
22. A savings account in which trust funds are deposited may be classified as a trust account of the salesperson.	**F** A savings account may be classified as a trust account of the brokerage, never the salesperson.
23. Licensees who avoid misrepresentation by acts of commission or omission are demonstrating competency.	**F** Integrity is one of the Cannons of Professional Ethics and Conduct. Integrity is demonstrated by avoiding misrepresentation by acts of commission or omission.
24. When negotiating a listing or offering to purchase the property as a result of a contract made while acting as an agent, a licensee must provide a property owner with an opinion of value.	**T**
25. A licensee may give an unexpected "thank you" merchant gift card up to $50 to an unlicensed person.	**T**
26. The Broker Responsibility Course content may be prescribed by accredited real estate schools.	**F** The Commission prescribes the title, content, and duration of the Broker Responsibility Course.
27. Complaints against a salesperson or a corporation are complaints against the sponsoring or designated broker.	**T**
28. Brokers may split fees with a negotiating nonresident broker.	**F** Brokers may share their fees with other brokers as long as the nonresident broker does not conduct negotiations in Texas.
29. Licensees may *NOT* discriminate against the protected classes of race, color, religion, age, sex, national origin, ancestry, familial status, or handicap individuals.	**F** Age is not a protected class.

30. If the license acquires ownership of money in the trust account, the money must be removed within 10 days.

F   If the license acquires ownership of money in the trust account, the money must be removed within 30 days.

31. Licensees may share any amount of their commission with a principal to the transaction.

T

32. When inactive licensees are selling or purchasing their own real estate, they are *NOT* obligated to disclose to the other party that they hold a real estate license.

F   All parties must be given disclosure of the licensee's license so there is no misleading or unfair advantage.

33. A licensee may *NOT* induce a party to a contract to break the contract for a substitution of a new contract.

T

34. It would be the unauthorized practice of law for a real estate licensee to advise the purchasers in writing to have an abstract of title examined by an attorney and obtain a policy of title insurance.

F   Licensees are required to advise the purchasers in writing before the closing of a real estate transaction to have an abstract of title examined by an attorney and obtain a policy of title insurance.

35. Licensees may assist a seller when selling real estate by lottery.

F   It is illegal for licensees to be involved in the transfer of real property through a lottery.

36. An investment entity may pay a finder's fee to anyone who provides a qualified lead.

F   A finder's fee cannot be paid to an unlicensed individual.

37. A licensee may *NOT* add factual details to the contract form if there is an addendum, lease, or other form promulgated or approved by the Commission.

T

38. Licensees may discourage legal advice.

F   Licensees must advise the principals that the instrument they are about to execute is binding and to seek legal advice before signing or initialing the contractual forms if they do not understand any of the provisions of the form.

39.	Fidelity, integrity, and competency are among the fiduciary duties owed by an agent to a client.	**F** The fiduciary duties owed by an agent to a client are obedience, loyalty, disclosure, confidentiality, accounting, and reasonable care. Fidelity, integrity, and competency are among the canons in the Canons of Professional Ethics and Conduct.
40.	Licensees may at their own discretion exclude all or a portion of a paragraph in the contract form that may benefit their principal.	**F** Licensees may only strike or add statements as desired by the principals and that are necessary to conform the instrument to the intent of the parties.
41.	To collect a commission through litigation, the seller's broker is required to prove the buyer was aware of the commission amount.	**F** The buyer's knowledge of the listing commission is irrelevant to the dispute between the listing broker and the seller.
42.	Brokers whose licensee fails to advise the purchasers in writing to have an abstract of title examined by an attorney and obtain a policy of title insurance at or prior to closing cannot collect a commission on the sale.	**T**
43.	Real estate licensees must identify themselves through the name of the brokerage or identify themselves as a listing associate in an advertisement.	**T**
44.	Salespersons are allowed to have their own website with all the office listings and only the salesperson's information.	**F** The salesperson is allowed to have a website with all the brokerage listings; however, the salesperson must include the name and contact information of the brokerage on each page.
45.	If the licensee discovers that the option fee check has been dishonored by the bank, the licensee must immediately notify only the person who wrote the check.	**F** If the licensee discovers that the option fee check has been dishonored by the bank, the licensee must immediately notify all parties.
46.	A licensee has "reasonable time" to respond to the Commission regarding documents pertaining to a consumer's written complaint. The Commission considers "reasonable time" to be within 24 hours after a request has been made.	**F** "Reasonable time" for the Commission means 10 working days from receipt of a request.
47.	Brokers must notify the Commission within 10 days after they stop using an assumed name in business.	**F** The broker has 30 days to notify the Commission.

48. Licensees are prohibited from soliciting listings from the owner who is under an exclusive listing agreement with another brokerage.

T

49. A real estate broker's license is *NOT* required for a person who agrees to negotiate a trade for another for a fee.

F To be able to receive a fee for negotiating the trading of properties requires a license.

50. The statement "a broker must be employed to recover a commission for services" means that the broker must work in a real estate office.

F The statement "a broker must be employed to recover a commission for services" means the seller must have signed the listing agreement to pay a commission to the broker for selling the property.

51. It is unlawful for a person to act in the capacity of or claim to be a real estate broker without first obtaining an office in an area zoned commercial.

F A broker's office can be in a home, as long as it does not violate zoning or deed restrictions.

52. The Texas Real Estate License Act stipulates that a broker will be liable if a salesperson fails to disclose that an owner has AIDS.

F Licensees are never to inquire about, discuss, or disclose persons who may have or have had HIV or AIDS.

53. A real estate salesperson may share the commission with any licensed attorney who has participated in the negotiations of the transaction.

F Texas attorneys may only receive compensation from the broker if the attorney is also a real estate broker or a licensee associated with a real estate broker.

54. Once TREC receives the newly licensed salesperson's sponsorship form from the sponsoring broker, the licensee may begin to practice real estate.

F A licensee may not engage in the real estate brokerage business until the sponsoring broker has received the salesperson's real estate license.

55. A salesperson may receive a commission from any real estate broker.

F A salesperson may receive a commission only from the broker who sponsored the salesperson at the time the commission was earned.

56. In order for a business entity to engage in real estate brokerage, at *LEAST* one officer of the business entity must be licensed as a broker.

F In order for a business entity to engage in real estate brokerage the entity plus at least one managing officer, acting as the designated broker, must be licensed as brokers.

57. A broker must obtain a branch office license for each additional office the broker maintains.

T

58. Placing escrow money in a licensee's operating account constitutes conversion.

F Commingling is when someone else's money is placed in a personal account. Conversion is spending someone else's money.

59. Commissions are set by the Texas Association of REALTORS®.

F Brokers may stipulate for their offices a set listing and buyer representation commission; otherwise, commissions are negotiable.

60. The Sherman Antitrust Act stipulates that commissions must be negotiable.

T

61. It is illegal for a broker to rebate a portion of the commission to the principal.

F It is legal for a broker to rebate a portion of the commission to the principal.

62. It is legal for a broker to rebate a portion of the commission to the principal for a real estate service, such as a referral.

F A broker may not rebate a portion of the commission to the principal for a real estate service, such as a referral.

IV. AGENCY/BROKERAGE

(Test Questions: Salesperson, 8; Broker, 10)

1. The TREC approved form Information About Brokerage Services is a voluntary form containing language mandated by TRELA.

   T

2. All disclosures of representation must be written disclosures.

   F The disclosure may be written or oral.

3. Third parties are owed fiduciary duties.

   F Fiduciary duties are owed only to an agent's client. The duties owed to a third party are honesty, fair dealings, and disclosure of material facts related to property condition.

4. When practicing intermediary brokerage, the salesperson may disclose information about one party to the other party if appointments are made.

   F During intermediary, the licensees may not disclose information about one party to the other party.

5. The broker must always make appointments if there are two or more associates in the brokerage.

   F The broker may, but is not required to, make appointments.

6. Confidentiality is the one fiduciary duty that remains forever, even after the representation has ended.

   T

7. When representing both parties in the same transaction, the broker can choose between dual agency and intermediary.

   F If the broker represents both parties in the same transaction, the brokerage must practice intermediary. Texas law does not recognize dual agency.

8. While working with a buyer, an associate of the listing broker gives advice and opinions to the buyer. MOST likely, the broker would be considered a single agent of the seller.

   F By giving advice and opinions to the buyer, an implied agency relationship was most likely created with the buyer in addition to the expressed agency relationship created in the listing agreement with the seller. This puts the broker in an illegal, nondisclosed, noncensual position of representing both parties.

9. Intermediary brokers may appoint themselves to one of the parties if there is only one other associate in the brokerage.

   F Brokers may never appoint themselves to either party.

10. In a real estate transaction involving intermediary brokerage, if one of the parties is related to a licensee, full disclosure must be given to all parties in the transaction.

    T

11.	The licensee is only required to disclose representation one time per transaction.	**F**	If representation changes during the transaction, new disclosure of the change must be given immediately.
12.	The Information About Brokerage Services form can be used as a representation agreement.	**F**	The Information About Brokerage Services form is not a representation agreement. It is information about the types of brokerage services available to the consumer.
13.	The Information About Brokerage Services form must be given at first contact.	**F**	The Information About Brokerage Services form is mandatory at first substantive dialog.
14.	First substantive dialogue is defined as any discussion regarding the property.	**F**	First substantive dialogue is a meeting or written communication that involves a substantive discussion relating to specific property.
15.	Appointed licensees may give advice and opinions to the party they have been appointed to during intermediary.	**T**	
16.	The parties may give permission orally or in writing for the brokerage to practice intermediary.	**F**	Under Texas law, the broker must have written consent from both parties before intermediary can begin.
17.	The broker is required to disclose to both parties the source of expected compensation in an intermediary transaction.	**T**	
18.	If there are appointments in an intermediary transaction, they must be in writing and given to both parties.	**T**	
19.	An independent contractor agreement is typically between the broker and an unlicensed assistant.	**F**	The independent contractor agreement is between the sponsoring broker and a licensed associate.
20.	MOST real estate salespeople are employees of the sponsoring broker.	**F**	Most real estate salespeople are independent contractors.
21.	A requirement to establish independent contractor status is that income is based on hours worked.	**F**	An independent contractor's income is not based on the number of hours worked.
22.	A broker who has only one associate salesperson may NOT act as an intermediary.	**F**	A broker who has only one affiliated license holder may act as an intermediary but may not make appointments.

23. A licensee does *NOT* have to provide the Information About Brokerage Services form to a party who is already represented by another licensee.	T
24. A salesperson could be an independent contractor or an employee.	T
25. A licensed salesperson or broker may sue to collect compensation.	F Only the broker of record may file suit for non-payment of commissions.
26. The brokerage may *NOT* receive any commission if there was failure to advise the buyer in writing regarding having an abstract of title examined by an attorney or getting title insurance.	T
27. Licensees are required to disclose whom the brokerage represents to all consumers at first contact.	T
28. All independent contractors are responsible for paying their own Social Security and income taxes.	T
29. Unintentional dual representation can occur when a licensee acts as a buyer or a seller.	T
30. Disputes relating to commissions between REALTORS® are settled by TREC.	F Broker-to-broker disputes are settled by the grievance committee through the board of REALTORS® or through the courts. TREC does not settle commission disputes.
31. A salesperson may receive a bonus directly from a client.	F All commissions belong to the sponsoring broker. It is the broker who shares commissions with the salesperson.
32. A broker should develop company policies that outline duties that can or cannot be performed and how commissions will be dispersed during intermediary.	T
33. The fiduciary duties owed to customers are loyalty, obedience, disclosure, accounting, confidentiality, and reasonable care and skill.	F Clients, not customers, receive fiduciary duties.
34. To put the client's interest above the licensee's interest is known as obedience.	F Loyalty is placing the interest of the client above the interest of the licensee.
35. Only during intermediary with appointments may advice and opinions be given to clients.	T
36. While employed by a real estate broker, a salesperson has the authority to act as an agent for the seller.	F While employed by a real estate broker, a salesperson has the authority to assume responsibilities assigned by the broker. It would be the broker who is the seller's agent. The salesperson would be acting as an agent of the broker.
37. Brokers may control what independent contractors do, but they cannot dictate how to do it.	T

38. When a broker associate joins a brokerage, TREC will issue an associate broker license to the associated broker.

    F   The broker associate will work under the guidance of the sponsoring broker.

39. Unlicensed personal assistants hired by licensees carry out limited functions that do *NOT* require a real estate license.

    T

40. An unlicensed assistant can show properties.

    F   The unlicensed assistant can open the door to the property and give brochures of the property to perspective buyers.

41. A broker whose licensee failed to advise a buyer to have an abstract of title examined by an attorney or get title insurance may have his license revoked.

    T

42. TREC requires a sponsoring broker to directly supervise a sponsored salesperson acting as an independent contractor.

    F   Sponsoring brokers are responsible for the actions of a salesperson the broker sponsors, whether the salesperson is an employee or independent contractor. However, they are not required to either directly or indirectly supervise a salesperson.

43. The one fiduciary duty that is easiest to perform during intermediary is confidentiality.

    F   Accounting, also known as disbursing of funds according to the parties' written agreement, is the easiest fiduciary duty to follow during intermediary.

44. A principal is also known as a customer of the broker.

    F   A principal is also known as a client of the broker.

45. The sponsoring broker is *NOT* responsible for an infraction by an associated licensee unless the broker is aware of the infraction.

    F   The sponsoring broker is responsible for all licensees in the brokerage regardless of the knowledge of the broker.

46. A salesperson is the general agent of the broker; the broker is the special agent of the client.

    T

47. Offers must be presented to the seller in the order that they are received.

    F   Offers are to be submitted to the seller simultaneously or as soon as possible.

48. The disclosure of any death on a property because of suicide is required under TRELA.

    F   There is no duty to disclose a death that occurred on a property by natural causes, suicide, or accident unrelated to the condition of the property under TRELA.

49. If the seller is aware of an endangered species on the property, full disclosure must be given.

T

50. The term "client" is defined by TRELA.

F   The term "client" is not defined by TRELA.

51. A gratuitous agency may pursue the commission from the client.

F   The agency relationship created when the agent provides brokerage services and charges no fee is known as gratuitous agency.

52. The verbiage "represents" means there is written agreement for the brokerage to act for the best interest of the client.

F   When the agent speaks, listens, and acts for the interest of the principal, this is the very essence of the word "represents."

53. Whoever pays the commission is the principal.

F   The payment of commissions does not constitute an agency agreement. It is most protective for both the client and the broker to have a written representation agreement with compensation addressed in the agreement.

54. A broker who is not compensated for services is *NOT* liable.

F   The broker is responsible for all real estate practice performed by the licensees of the brokerage, regardless of a commission.

55. An implied agency with the buyer can result if the words and conduct of the salesperson do *NOT* dispel this assumption.

T

56. An in-house sale is also known as an intermediary transaction.

F   An in-house sale may have the seller as a client and the buyer as customer, or vice versa. "In-house" refers to only one broker involved in the transaction; however, both parties may not both be clients.

57. Brokers are mandated to have benefits for independent contractors, as well as employees.

F   Brokers are not obligated to have benefits for either party.

58. The principal broker of a firm is responsible for the actions of every licensee affiliated with and acting for the real estate brokerage firm.

T

59. Competency is the obligation of the real estate agent to be knowledgeable, informed on market conditions and laws, and exercise judgment and skill in the performance of the work performed.

T

60.	An unlicensed assistant may *NOT* set appointments to show a listing.	**F** An unlicensed assistant may call a homeowner and schedule an appointment for the licensee to bring a potential buyer to see the property.
61.	The minimum services requirement of TRELA requires a limited services provider to inform the client if material infor-mation related to the trans-action is received by the broker.	**T**
62.	A limited services provider may instruct another broker to negotiate directly with the client.	**F** A limited services provider may not instruct another broker to negotiate directly with the client.
63.	It would be appropriate use of an unlicensed assistant to answer phone calls, maintain records, handle correspondence, schedule appointments, and serve as host or hostess at open houses.	**T**
64.	An unlicensed assistant may *NOT* engage in any activity for which a license is required.	**T**

V.   CONTRACTS

(Test questions: Salesperson, 7; Broker, 8)

1.	When selling the property "as is," the seller has no duty to disclose defects on the property.	**F** The seller and the brokerage must disclose all known material facts relating to the property.
2.	A seller conceals previous water damage. The listing licensee is unable to see that there was previous damage. Under TRELA, the licensee is responsible for failing to disclose the damage.	**F** The brokerage is not responsible unless the licensee knowingly concealed the material fact.
3.	A Seller's Disclosure Notice does *NOT* have to be given when a property is transferred by foreclosure.	**T**
4.	If the structure on a property has a value of less than 10% of the total property, the owner of the property is exempt from delivering a seller's disclosure of property condition.	**F** If the value of the structure on a property does not exceed 5% of the total property value, the owner of the property is exempt from delivering a seller's disclosure of property condition.
5.	Builders must give some form of property disclosure to the prospective buyer.	**F** An owner of a single-family dwelling that has never been occupied is exempt from the seller's disclosure of property condition.
6.	A landlord who has never resided in a property is exempt from giving the buyer a seller's disclosure notice of property condition.	**F** A landlord is not exempt from delivering a seller's disclosure notice.
7.	A material fact is any fact that is relevant to a person making a decision.	**T**
8.	Licensees must disclose the locations of registered sex offenders.	**F** Information about the location of registered sex offenders does not have to be disclosed in relation to a single-family home, but neither is it prohibited.
9.	TREC rules prohibit the disclosure, discussions, and inquiries regarding AIDS and HIV.	**T**
10.	When asked by the seller principal *NOT* to disclose the rusted drip pan, the licensee would be obligated to follow the instructions of the seller client because of the fiduciary duties owed to a principal.	**F** A licensee who withholds material facts may be guilty of misrepresentation or fraud.

11. The stigma of the presence of asbestos has been reduced because of better knowledge and understanding of remedies. Therefore, it is no longer a mandatory material fact.

F The presence of asbestos requires disclosure to potential buyers. It is addressed in the TREC's Seller's Disclosure of Property Condition form.

12. If the seller does *NOT* deliver the required Seller's Disclosure of Property Condition form on or before the effective date of an executory contract, the buyer may sue for specific performance.

F The buyer may terminate the contract within seven days after receiving the notice or before closing, whichever is earlier.

13. The seller, seller's brokerage, and buyer's brokerage has no duty to release information related to a death by suicide on the property.

T

14. A property that has had a death occur on the property is known as a stigmatized property.

T

15. A broker may use a different seller's disclosure form than the TREC-approved form.

T

16. The disclosure of a municipal utility district (MUD) is *NOT* necessary because there are addenda that address this issue.

F The material fact disclosure of a MUD is addressed on the Seller's Disclosure of Property Condition, and there are two addenda that give the buyer detailed information.

17. During the listing presentation, the listing associate asks the sellers whether the property has an attic fan. The correct response would be for the associate to look for an attic fan so that the sellers can fill out the disclosure notice honestly.

F The correct response would be for the sellers to fill out the form to the best of their knowledge, marking yes, no, or unknown.

18. TREC has a mandatory seller's disclosure form.

F TREC has an approved form that is voluntary for use.

19. The TREC Seller's Disclosure of Property Condition is a promulgated form.

F The form is approved, but it is not promulgated.

20. The seller is only liable for nondisclosure of the items on the seller's disclosure form.

F All material facts must be disclosed, including facts that may not be addressed in the seller's disclosure form.

21. Environmental hazards are a material fact.

T

22. Promulgated forms may be reproduced as printed copies made from copies obtained from TREC.

T

23. There are seven promulgated sales contract forms.

F There are six TREC-promulgated sales contract forms.

24.	Only the Farm and Ranch Contract addresses reservation of mineral rights.	**F** TREC has an addendum that can be attached to any sales contract that addresses mineral rights.
25.	A buyer may make an agreement contingent upon the sale of another property by writing the contingency in special provisions of the contract.	**F** There is an addendum that must be attached at the time of offer; it is the Addendum for Sale of Other Property by Buyer.
26.	If the seller decides to assist the buyer in financing, the parties would use an amendment of seller financing.	**F** The parties would use an addendum of seller financing.
27.	Builders must use the TREC-promulgated forms for the sale of their properties when a licensee is involved in the sale.	**F** Sellers have the legal right to use any sales contract form that they want.
28.	The only place in the sales contract that the legal phrase "time is of the essence" is located is in the finance paragraph (4).	**F** In all the TREC promulgated sales contracts, the legal phrase "time is of the essence" is located in the option of termination paragraph (23).
29.	"Time is of the essence" means that the parties are allowed to unconditionally waive the time frame.	**F** "Time is of the essence" means that strict compliance with the time agreed upon in the contract must be adhered to by both parties.
30.	An amendment is a change or modification to the existing content of a contract.	**T**
31.	An addendum contains additional information that is part of the contract.	**T**
32.	TREC contract forms must be used by real estate licensees for all real estate transactions.	**F** TREC contract forms must be used by real estate licensees in all transactions to which the forms are applicable, unless one of the exceptions defined by statute applies.
33.	An option to purchase contract is a unilateral contract.	**T**
34.	TREC drafts and revises contract forms and then promulgates them for use in real property transactions.	**F** The Broker-Lawyer Committee drafts and revises contract forms for licensee usage. The forms are then either promulgated or approved by TREC.

35. A unilateral contract exists when a promise is exchanged for a promise.

F A bilateral contract exists when a promise is exchanged for a promise.

36. A triple net lease consists of a base amount plus the lessee paying taxes, insurance, and maintenance on the property.

T

37. The salesperson's name and logo may be printed outside the border at the bottom of each contractual page.

F The broker's name may be inserted in any blank provided for that purpose. The broker's name and logo may be printed outside the border at the top of each contractual page.

38. An independent contractor agreement is known as a unilateral contract.

F An independent contractor agreement is a bilateral agreement. It contains promises in exchange for promises between the broker and the licensed associate.

39. The vendor is known as the buyer.

F The vendor is known as the seller.

40. The vendee is known as the seller.

F The vendee is the buyer.

41. The Seller's Temporary Residential Lease is the only lease TREC promulgates and is used when the buyer moves into the property before closing.

F There are two temporary lease agreements promulgated by TREC. The Seller's Temporary Residential Lease is used when the seller remains in the property after closing. The Buyer's Temporary Residential Lease is used when the buyer moves in before closing.

42. Under the statute of frauds, all leases of one year or longer must be in writing to be enforceable.

F Leases that are for more than one year must be in writing to be enforceable under the statute of frauds.

43. An oral sales contract for real property is illegal.

F Oral contracts for the sale of real estate are not illegal, but because of the statute of frauds, oral contracts are unenforceable.

44. The purpose of the statute of frauds is to prevent fraudulent oral evidence of a fictitious contract from being enforced.

T

45. In Texas, contracts for the sale of real estate generally assume that time is of the essence.

F Without a "time is of the essence" clause, Texas courts assume a "reasonable time."

46. In the event of the seller's default, the buyer may enforce specific performance, seek such other relief as may be provided by law, or both, or terminate the contract and receive the earnest money, thereby releasing both parties from the contract.

T

47. The buyer has two business days after effective date of the contract to deliver the option fee to the seller or the seller's brokerage.

F The buyer has two days, holidays and weekend days included, to deliver the option fee to the seller or the seller's brokerage.

48. Only the spouse who is on the deed needs to sign a contract for the sale of real estate to transfer homestead property.

F Both spouse's signatures must be on all the contractual documents when the property is classified as a homestead.

49. All joint tenants must sign a contract for the sale of real estate.

T

50. The parol evidence rule states that oral agreements pertaining to real property made by the parties before entering into a written contract may be used in the court to dispute the written provisions expressed in the contract.

F The parol evidence rule provides for evidence that is outside and separate from the written contractual agreement and that is not admissible into court.

51. The law providing that the seller bear any loss because of destruction of the property before settlement is called the Uniform Vendor and Purchaser Risk Act.

T

52. Earnest money is the consideration in the contractual agreement between parties.

F Earnest money is not the consideration. The sales price and the promise given in exchange for a promise is adequate consideration to bind a purchase agreement.

53. Earnest money is required for a contract to be valid.

F Earnest money is not required in a real property contract agreement.

54. Liquidated damages are the same as money damages.

F Liquidated damages are the same as earnest money.

55. If the seller defaults, the buyer can ask for the earnest money or sue for specific performance but can do nothing else.

F If the seller defaults, the buyer can ask for the earnest money or sue for specific performance and/or other remedies provided by law.

56. The statute of limitations to bring suit against a party is two years for a written contract of sale of real property.

F The statute of limitations to bring suit against a party is two years for an oral contract and four years for a written contract.

57. The buyer and the seller have agreed to have an option time of 15 days for $1,500. The seller must receive the $1,500 no later than the expiration of the 15-day period.

F The buyer must pay the seller or the listing office the $1,500 no later than the end (11:59 pm) of the second day after effective date of the contract.

58. Earnest money and option money are the same.

F Earnest money is applied to the sales price and can be a remedy of the seller if the buyer is in default. Option money is paid to the seller for the buyer to have an unconditional right to terminate the contract within a specific time frame.

59. If the seller fails to deliver the title commitment to the buyer within the time provided, through no fault of the seller, the buyer may extend the time up to 15 days.

T

60. If any part of the property is damaged or destroyed by fire or other casualty after the effective date of this contract, the seller may terminate the contract.

F The buyer, not the seller, may terminate the contract.

61. All sales contracts for real property must be in writing to be enforceable.

T

VI.   SPECIAL TOPICS

(Test questions: Salesperson 4; Broker 6)

1. All of a spouse's property, both real and personal, owned or claimed before marriage is community property.

    F Both real and personal property owned before marriage is separate property.

2. All real property acquired during marriage by gift or will is community property.

    F Property acquired during marriage by gift or will is separate property.

3. Separate property may become community property if it is commingled with community property or if community funds are used to maintain the separate property.

    T

4. Income received from separate property remains separate.

    F Income from separate property is community property unless there is a separate written agreement stating differently.

5. Bob has separate property that he acquired before marrying Betty. While Bob was out of the country on business, Betty paid the taxes on all the properties with the income from Bob's separate property, which Bob and Betty contractually agreed would be treated as Bob's separate property. Bob's separate property remains separate.

    T

6. Susan was given her grandmother's dining table, 12 chairs, and a hutch. In the divorce, her husband has rights to the dining room furniture because it was part of their marital home furnishings.

    F Property acquired by gift is separate property unless there is a written agreement of the parties stipulating something different.

7. Texas is one of the eight community property states.

    F There are nine community property states. They are Arizona, California, Idaho, Louisiana, Nevada, New Mexico, Texas, Washington, and Wisconsin.

8. Joe moved into Alice's condo. Later that year, they married. Alice's condo is separate property.

    T

9. Joe moved into Alice's condo. Later that year they married. When Alice sells her condo, only Alice must sign the listing agreement because Joe's name is *NOT* on the title.

    F Even though Joe's name is not on the title, he has resided in the property and will need to be on the listing agreement, contract of sale, and sign a waiver of all rights and interest of the property at closing.

10. Joe moved into Alice's condo. Later that year, they married. Upon closing, the proceeds are community property funds.

    F Unless there is a separate written agreement between Joe and Alice, the funds are the separate property of Alice.

11. The homestead property is exempt from a defaulted hospital bill.

    T

12.	The homestead value that is exempt from creditors' claims is defined by federal law.	**F** State laws define homestead exemption rights.
13.	The benefits of homestead laws are transferred according to the will.	**F** The state homestead laws establish the rights of the surviving spouse, regardless of the will.
14.	Minor children have the same homestead rights as the deceased parent.	**T**
15.	Homestead rights are protected against adverse possession.	**F** The homestead property must be occupied as the primary residence; therefore, adverse possession would not be possible.
16.	A single person can have up to 200 acres as a homestead exemption for a rural property.	**F** A single person may have up to 100 acres as a homestead in a rural area.
17.	Both families and single persons can claim up to 10 acres as a homestead exemption for urban properties.	**T**
18.	Upon the death of Darla's father, the will vested the devised property to her instead of her stepmother; therefore, her stepmother must leave the property or pay rent.	**F** Darla's stepmother is protected under the homestead laws and cannot be forced to move, sell, or pay rent.
19.	Ownership and occupancy as the principal place of residence automatically creates the homestead.	**T**
20.	A homestead exemption protects the property from foreclosure because of a tax default.	**F** Homestead exemption properties are protected from general creditors. They are not protected from mortgage, deed of trust, tax, HOA, mechanics' or materialmen's liens, or foreclosures.
21.	The purpose of the Deceptive Trade Practices Act is to protect consumers from hidden finance charges.	**F** Regulation Z protects consumers from hidden finance charges.
22.	The consumer has until the first year from the date of discovery to file a DTPA suit.	**F** The consumer has two years from the date of discovery to file a DTPA suit.
23.	Treble damages are automatic if the conduct of the defendant was found as intentional.	**T**
24.	The Deceptive Trade Practices Act protects consumers from false, misleading, and deceptive business practices and provides efficient and economical procedures to secure such protection.	**T**
25.	A consumer who is represented by legal counsel may waive the right to bring suit under the DTPA.	**T**
26.	Recovery of damages under the DTPA is limited to economic damages unless the defendant is found to have committed the act knowingly, then damages for mental anguish may also be awarded.	**T**

27. Consumers are encouraged to sign a waiver stating that they would have no rights to sue under DTPA.	F Waivers are against public policy and are generally unenforceable under the Texas Business and Commerce Code.
28. The listing office advertised that the roof is new. The seller disclosed in the seller's disclosure that the shingles were replaced two months before listing the property. The listing office and the seller would *NOT* be liable under DTPA because disclosure was made to all parties before the contract.	F The listing office, broker, and listing associate deceived the buyer by stating that the roof was replaced when in fact only the shingles were replaced.
29. Property acquired during marriage by gift is considered community property.	F Property acquired during marriage by gift is considered separate property.
30. Property acquired during marriage by devise or descent is considered community property.	F Property acquired during marriage by devise or descent is considered separate property.
31. John died with a will. Therefore it is the same as saying John died intestate.	F Intestate is when one dies without a will. Testate is when one dies with a will.
32. When John died without a will, he was survived by his wife and their two children, ages 8 and 10, as well as an adult child from a previous relationship. John's wife has all rights and interest to the homestead property.	F Because there was no will and John had a child from a previous marriage, the courts through decent and distribution will divide the interest of the property between John's wife and John's children.
33. Property acquired during marriage by personal injury lawsuit is considered separate property.	T
34. Upon the death of a person leaving a will, the real property is devised to the devisees.	T
35. Upon the death of a person *NOT* leaving a will, the real property descends to the heirs.	T
36. The seller's husband died leaving all real and personal property to the wife. Before the wife can list the property, the will must be prorated.	T
37. A testator is one who is named as the devisee.	F A person who makes a will is the testator.
38. A property owner died testate, leaving all real property to his granddaughter. The estate passes to the granddaughter immediately upon the property owner's death.	T
39. The broker is entitled to a commission when a ready, willing, and able buyer goes under contract to purchase a property.	T
40. An heir is one who receives real property from a will.	F A devisee receives real property from a will.
41. A landlord may file a lien for unpaid rent that attaches to nonexempt property.	T

42. The security deposit may be applied to the last month's rent.

F The security deposit may not be used by the tenant for the last month's rent.

43. In a commercial property, the security deposit must be returned or accounted for on or before the 30th day after the tenant surrenders the property.

F The landlord has 60 days to account for or to surrender the security deposit to the commercial tenant.

44. If the tenant leaves no forwarding address, the landlord can keep all the security deposit.

T

45. The security deposit may be applied to unpaid rent, cleaning of the property, or repairs.

F The security deposit may not be applied to cleaning of the property.

46. A security deposit is a payment by a tenant, held by the landlord during the lease term, and kept (wholly or partially) on default, or on destruction of the premises by the tenant.

T

47. The residential landlord must account for the security deposit no later than the 30th day after the tenant vacates the property.

T

48. Bill is purchasing a single-family residence that has a tenant with three months left on the lease. Bill must give the tenant a 30-day notice that the lease will end after closing of the sale.

F A property that has a tenant with a valid lease at the time of the sale of the property has the right to continue possession of the property until the termination of the lease.

49. The landlord must rekey the property for each tenant before the new tenant moves into the property.

F The landlord must rekey the locks at each tenant turnover. The landlord has until the end of the seventh day from the day the new tenant moves into the property.

50. Bill is purchasing a single-family residence that has a tenant with three months left on the lease. At closing, the security deposit is a credit of the seller and a debit of the buyer.

F The security deposit is a debit of the seller and a credit of the buyer at the time of funding.

51. The debtor must have at *LEAST* 21 days to cure the default before the property is posted as a foreclosure.

F The debtor must have at least 20 days to cure the default before notice of the sale can be given.

52. Sales of properties on the courthouse step take place on the second Tuesday of every month.

F Courthouse foreclosure sales are on the first Tuesday of every month.

53. Sales of properties on the courthouse step take place at the federal courthouse.

F The sales takes place at the county courthouse in the county in which the land is located.

54. There is no statutory redemption period for a property foreclosed on for nonpayment of a deed of trust loan.

T

55. A condominium that was foreclosed on because of nonpayment of assessment dues has a statutory redemption period of 180 days.

   F   The owner of a condominium facing foreclosure because of the default of assessment dues has 90 days to redeem the property from the date of the sale.

56. The highest bidder must allow for a two-year right of redemption for a property that was acquired through a defaulted tax foreclosure.

   T

57. The high bidder for a property that was acquired through a defaulted tax foreclosure receives a limited warranty deed.

   F   The high bidder receives a sheriff's deed or a sheriff's certificate of sale.

58. Before a foreclosure, a defaulting borrower may pay off debt plus interest and reclaim the home under the equitable right of redemption.

   T

59. A property waiting for foreclosure to take place can be sold as a short sale.

   T

60. The term "short sale" reflects the sales price typically being less that the loan amount.

   T

61. Constructive notice is also known as direct knowledge.

   F   Actual notice is also known as direct knowledge.

62. Constructive notice means not only that information is available for review but also that someone has been given the information.

   F   Actual notice means not only that information is available for review but also that someone has been given the information.

63. Tenants may record their right of possession to a property.

   T

64. Anthony sells a portion of property to Betty, who records the deed in the county clerk's office. If Anthony tries to sell the same portion of property to Carla, constructive notice of the prior sale will be given because Betty promptly recorded the deed.

   T

65. All deeds must be recorded to have validity.

   F   Recording a deed is not essential for validity.

66. When a purchaser has a title search done, it shows whether there are any liens on the property and who is listed on the chain of title.

   T

67. A title report is the same as an abstract of title.

   F   A title report shows only the current state of the title, along with the recorded objections. An abstract of title is a full summary of all consecutive grants, conveyances, wills, records, and judicial proceedings that affect the title.

68. The history of deeds is an abstract of title.

   F   The history of deeds or conveyances is known as the chain of title.

69. A document that is acknowledged is also referred to as notarized.

   T

70. The cost of an owner's title policy is paid either at closing or can be rolled into the monthly payment of the loan.

   F   The title policy is paid one time at the closing of the sale.

71. Default on covenants, conditions, and restrictions can lead to a general lien.	F A default in dues associated with the covenants, conditions, and restrictions can lead to a specific lien.
72. The developer of a subdivision typically stipulates the restrictive covenants.	T
73. An encumbrance is anything (such as a mortgage, tax, or judgment lien; an easement; or a restriction on the use of the land) that may diminish the value or use and enjoyment of a property.	T
74. A mechanic's lien is a general lien.	F A mechanic's lien is a specific lien.
75. A lien is an encumbrance on a property.	T
76. To be entitled to a mechanic's lien, the provider must have worked under contract with the owner or the owner's authorized representative.	T
77. If the property is a homestead, both spouses must sign a contract for a valid mechanic's lien to be filed.	T
78. A mechanic's lien would be available to subcontractors, contractors, and surveyors.	T
79. A lien on a property acts as security of a debt.	T
80. The Texas Land Board is unique in that it is the only type of veteran's land loan available in the United States.	T
81. Texas veterans have two 100% loans available to them, the Veterans Affairs loan and the Texas Land Board loan.	F Texas veterans are required to put down a minimum of 5% for the down payment.
82. The VA loan is available to all spouses of veterans.	F The VA loan is available to spouses of veterans who have died in the line of duty.
83. Insufficient sale proceeds in a foreclosure may entitle the lender to seek a deficiency judgment, unless otherwise prohibited by law. Action to obtain the judgment must be commenced within two years of the foreclosure sale.	T
84. Upon receipt of the final payment, the contractor must furnish a final-bills-paid affidavit.	T
85. Nonjudicial foreclosure is allowed when the deed of trust contains an acceleration clause.	F Nonjudicial foreclosure is allowed when the deed of trust contains a power of sale clause.
86. The seller has the right to choose the title company if the seller is paying the title policy.	F The seller may suggest the title company; however, it is the borrower of a federally influenced loan that has the right to choose the title company, regardless of who pays for the title policy. (RESPA section 9)
87. The Texas Veterans Land Board has three loan programs used to assist Texas veterans in either purchasing a primary residence, land, or making home improvements.	T

88. The maximum loan under the Veterans Housing Assistance Program is capped at $500,000.

    F The maximum loan under the Veterans Housing Assistance Program is capped at $325,000.

89. A homeowners association lien is *NOT* enforceable against a homestead.

    F A homeowners association lien is enforceable against a homestead.

APPENDIX Self-Score Answer Sheets

Texas Exam Prep Self-Score Answer Sheet State Portion

Students taking the pre-test: Use this sheet to mark your answers as you take the test. Then grade your test and write the correct answer next to the questions you got wrong. Be sure to have this answer sheet with you during the course.

Students taking the post-test: Take the exam online, review it, and then record your answers on this sheet.

Student Name: _____

Test (circle one): _____ Pre-Test / Post-Test

Commission Duties and Powers (Salesperson, 2 questions / Broker, 3 questions)	Licensing (Salesperson, 2 questions / Broker, 4 questions)	Standards of Conduct (Salesperson, 7 questions / Broker, 9 questions)
1. _____ 2. _____	3. _____ 4. _____	5. _____ 6. _____ 7. _____ 8. _____ 9. _____ 10. _____ 11. _____

Agency and Brokerage (Salesperson, 8 questions / Broker, 10 questions)	Contracts (Salesperson, 7 questions / Broker, 8 questions)	*9+ Special Topics (Salesperson, 4 questions / Broker, 6 questions)
12. _____ 13. _____ 14. _____ 15. _____ 16. _____ 17. _____ 18. _____ 19. _____	20. _____ 21. _____ 22. _____ 23. _____ 24. _____ 25. _____ 26. _____	27. _____ 28. _____ 29. _____ 30. _____

Texas Exam Prep Self-Score Answer Sheet State Portion

Students taking the pre-test: Use this sheet to mark your answers as you take the test. Then grade your test and write the correct answer next to the questions you got wrong. Be sure to have this answer sheet with you during the course.

Students taking the post-test: Take the exam online, review it, and then record your answers on this sheet.

Student Name: _____

Test (circle one): _____ Pre-Test / Post-Test

Commission Duties and Powers (Salesperson, 2 questions / Broker, 3 questions)	Licensing (Salesperson, 2 questions / Broker, 4 questions)	Standards of Conduct (Salesperson, 7 questions / Broker, 9 questions)
1. _____ 2. _____	3. _____ 4. _____	5. _____ 6. _____ 7. _____ 8. _____ 9. _____ 10. _____ 11. _____

Agency and Brokerage (Salesperson, 8 questions / Broker, 10 questions)	Contracts (Salesperson, 7 questions / Broker, 8 questions)	*9+ Special Topics (Salesperson, 4 questions / Broker, 6 questions)
12. _____ 13. _____ 14. _____ 15. _____ 16. _____ 17. _____ 18. _____ 19. _____	20. _____ 21. _____ 22. _____ 23. _____ 24. _____ 25. _____ 26. _____	27. _____ 28. _____ 29. _____ 30. _____